JUST CHICKEN

Happy Holiday Honey 1988

JUST CHICKEN

THOMAS HINDE & CORDELIA CHITTY

BARRON'S
Woodbury, New York • London • Toronto • Sydney

Authors: Thomas Hinde (Sir Thomas Chitty), best known as a novelist, lives in Sussex, England. He has also written many books on gardening, self-sufficiency, natural history and country life. He and his daughter Cordelia Chitty have been cooking together for family and friends for many years.

Cartoonist: William Belcher

We would also like to thank the British Chicken Information Service for their help and support.

A PHOEBE PHILLIPS EDITIONS BOOK

First English language edition 1985 in the United States and its possessions, Canada, and the Philippine Islands by Barron's Educational Series, Inc.

Text copyright © Thomas Hinde and Cordelia Chitty 1985
Design and illustrations copyright © Phoebe Phillips Editions 1985

All rights reserved.
No part of this book may be reproduced in any form, by photostat, microfilm, xerography, or any other means, or incorporated into any information retrieval system, electronic or mechanical, without the written permission of the copyright owner.

All enquiries should be addressed to:
Barron's Educational Series, Inc.
113 Crossways Park Drive
Woodbury, New York 11797

Library of Congress Card No. 85-4030
International Standard Book Number 0-8120-3569-0

Library of Congress Cataloging in Publication Data
Hinde, Thomas, 1926-
  Just chicken.

  Includes index.
  1. Cookery (Chicken) I. Chitty, Cordelia.
II. Title.
TX750.H55 1985   641.6'65   85-4030
ISBN 0-8120-3569-0

Printed in Great Britain
5678   987654321

CONTENTS

Introduction 6
Kinds of Chicken 9
Choosing and Buying 10
Preparation 11
Basic Cooking Methods 16
Carving 18
Preserving 18
Soups 21
Pâtés and Hors d'oeuvre 33
Simple Dishes 43
Adventurous Dishes 61
Elaborate Dishes 83
Cold Dishes 105
Cooked Chicken Dishes 115
Index 126

INTRODUCTION

"Chicken makes the meal," the Spanish say. Long before I heard this I thought of chicken as something special. It arrived for lunch on occasional Sundays, in place of the usual fatty loin of pork, or tough roast beef. And it was cooked in just two ways: roast or boiled. I continue to think fondly of those great birds – six-pounders, at least, in my imagination – crisply brown with Brussels sprouts and roast potatoes, or creamy and tender, with brown gravy, and the fact that their present-day smaller relations have become the most economical food you can buy still seems something of a miracle.

During the War my family continued to be closely connected with chickens. Our roosters, hatched by the mother of the flock, a huge Rhode Island Red named Beauty, of course went into the pot. But so did any hen stupid enough to have a prolonged molt, or which began to "mope." Our aim was to forestall the later stages of a complaint which we unscientifically called "going light." I well remember my mother discovering how to turn such aged boilers into roasters by first simmering them for a couple of hours, then roasting them for an hour in a hot oven. One other dish she developed in those days of food rationing was Chicken Rice Casserole (see page 120), to make use of leftovers.

So it wasn't until my wife and I began to cook for ourselves in a more adventurous way, and later when our daughter, Cordelia, emerged from the cake-and-cookies period to join us, that we discovered the many other possibilities of chicken. The Spanish are right. Quite simply, it is by far the most adaptable of all meats.

The reasons are not hard to discover: the tenderness of the flesh of a young chicken – or even an old one when properly treated; the way in which this varies on any one bird, so that different parts have different characteristics and suit different dishes; above all, the fact that chicken meat does *not* itself have too strong a flavor, and as a result can be blended with such a wide variety of other flavors.

As if this were not enough, a chicken comes with a deliciously tender and flavorful liver, an excellent basis for a wide range of pâtés and terrines, and the stock you can make from chicken bones not only forms the basis of many of the best soups but is an important ingredient of a number of other dishes.

This book gathers together the discoveries which Cordelia and I have made. They range from simple stews to complicated creations like Broiled Chicken Maintenon (see page 92), developed by Louis XIV's chef in honor of the king's mistress. In selecting them we worked on two principles. The first was that they should be as varied as possible. Even now, we continue to be astonished at the way in which a new recipe can transform a basic frozen chicken into a totally new culinary experience. We include dishes from twenty-four countries.

The second was that each dish in its own way should be delicious. As a result, you will find a fair proportion of classic chicken dishes, from Coq au Vin (see page 102) to Paella (see page 89). But for these two in particular, as well as for many others, it took much research to discover a recipe that really works. Every one of them we have tested, most of them many times, and we try to explain our methods clearly and simply.

Neither of us has ever taken a cooking lesson (except from each other), and it is our belief that almost everyone can turn himself or herself into a competent cook provided they can read a cookbook and they enjoy the results. If this is true of cooking in general, it is particularly so of chicken cooking. One or two of our recipes take time, trouble and care, but none is really difficult in the way that the elaborate creations of pastry cooking could be said to be.

We have divided the main-course recipes according to their easiness or difficulty, rather than the time they take. One or two of the very simple ones need long, slow cooking. In the other sections you will find some dishes that could equally well be eaten as hot main courses – the two pies, for example – but we have separated them when, in our opinion, they are better cold, and because it may be convenient to find possible picnic dishes collected in one place.

The quantities we give for most of the recipes are enough to **serve four people,** unless otherwise noted. By using a larger bird and increasing the other ingredients proportionately, you can almost always extend the dish to serve six. For more than this we suggest using two chickens.

Spoon measurements for dry ingredients are very slightly rounded unless otherwise stated.

Whenever the oven is used it should be preheated. We have given the oven temperatures with the ingredients so that you will be able to see at a glance for which recipes you will need the oven. Sometimes it is not needed until nearly the end of the cooking time.

Occasionally, dishes require baking at very low temperatures. Our oven functions well at the temperatures given in these recipes, but do check the lowest temperature at which yours is efficient and use that. Also, test that the meat is cooked – just stick a skewer into it and make sure the juices are clear.

FOOD VALUE

As well as being the most adaptable of meats, chicken is one of the healthiest. It is low in calories, and it has less fat than beef, veal, pork, lamb or even turkey. The breast is the least fatty and the skin most fatty. A few of our recipes specifically require the skin, but for many others, even when we don't say so, the skin could be removed and discarded.

Chicken is also rich in protein and contains some of the B vitamins, and useful minerals. For all these reasons it is a favorite of those who need to lose weight but enjoy good food.

If you are concerned about cholesterol substitute a soft margarine for the butter we have specified for frying or for roasting or when making roux-based sauces.

Kinds of chicken

Poussin

A poussin is a very young chicken about 4-6 weeks of age and weighing from 1-2 pounds. Each bird will serve one or two people, depending on the size. Poussins should be fried, roasted or broiled. Young chickens of 10-12 weeks are also available. They weigh 2-3 pounds and give 3-4 servings. They can be roasted, fried or broiled. If unavailable, substitute game hens.

Broiler-fryer

Broiler-fryers are the most popular kind of chicken. They generally weigh between 2½-3½ pounds, are aged between 5 months and a year and will give about 4 servings. This kind of chicken can be casseroled, roasted, broiled or fried. Most chicken parts that are sold come from this kind of bird.

Boiling fowl or stewing hen
A boiling fowl or stewing hen is an older bird weighing about 4-7 pounds and giving 4-6 servings. It tends to be less popular nowadays, perhaps because it is tougher and it will have more fat. However, the ample meat has more flavor than that of a broiler-fryer and is extremely good if cooked by a slow, moist method such as poaching or casseroling.

Roaster
A larger chicken that is meant to be roasted and served whole. These average 5-7 pounds and serve about 6. They are juicy and mild flavored.

Grading chickens
All the chickens and chicken parts that you buy from the supermarket or butcher have been inspected by the Department of Agriculture to ensure that they have been raised and processed under sanitary conditions. Most birds will have been graded either USDA Grade A for the best-quality chickens or USDA Grade B for birds which are of less choice quality but still good and usually cheaper.

Choosing and buying

Frozen chickens
When buying these take the same reasonable precautions you would take when buying any frozen food. See that the bird's sell-by date (if given) has not passed, that the wrapper has not been damaged and that there are no discolored patches on the skin.

Fresh chickens
Most chickens sold as "fresh" have been reared by the same intensive farming methods as frozen chickens, but they should have a better flavor. Butchers and gourmet food stores may sell genuine "farmyard"

or free-range birds. Your best guide to quality is the reliability of the store or butcher you are buying from.

From the farm
If you live near a farm, you may be able to buy freshly killed chickens. Some egg-producing farms sell their laying hens when they have finished their first season, and these can be a bargain. They should be treated as old birds, and will have the good flavor of a stewing fowl. However, you may have to pluck and draw them yourself. To improve their quality, follow the practice of plucking and removing their intestines and crops, but leaving on their heads and feet and hanging them for 2 or 3 days, like game birds.

Chicken parts
Chicken parts are available fresh or frozen. They are convenient for dishes which call for a particular cut, but they are often not good value. It is better to buy a whole bird and use the parts not needed in one recipe in another dish.

Livers
Chicken livers can be bought either fresh or frozen. They are usually available in half-pound or one-pound packages. A single liver from one bird may not be of use on its own so keep a container of livers in the freezer and keep adding to it until you have enough to make a pâté.

Preparation

PLUCKING
Plucking is not difficult, although it is time-consuming, particularly if the bird was molting when it was killed and covered with feathers that have only

partly emerged. Chickens are easiest to pluck just after they have been killed, but this is not usually possible if you buy from a farm. To pluck, pull away the body feathers in tufts, pulling in the opposite direction to the way they lie naturally, then pull out the large wing and tail feathers, one at a time, using pliers if necessary. Finally, singe the body fluff.

DRAWING
1. Cut the feet off just below the knees.
2. Cut the head off about 3 inches from the shoulders.
3. Open and push back the skin around the remaining 3 inches of neck, and cut the neck off close to the shoulders, then remove the crop and windpipe.
4. With a sharp knife, cut around the vent, then cut the skin upward as far as the bottom end of the breastbone.
5. Insert your hand (wear a thin rubber glove if you feel a little squeamish) and pull out all the intestines together.
6. Separate and set aside the liver and heart, first cutting out and discarding the small green gall-sack, taking care not to break it. Its bitter contents can ruin the taste of any part of a chicken that it contaminates.
7. Slice the gizzard in half, wash out its contents and remove the tough, wrinkled inner skin. The flesh of the gizzard is edible and can, for example, be chopped and added to a stuffing, but it is usually best simmered with the neck and bones for stock.
8. Wipe the chicken inside and out with a damp cloth.

THAWING
The usual advice given is that a 3-3½ pound frozen chicken must be allowed at least 24 hours to thaw in a refrigerator or about 8 hours at room temperature, longer if your kitchen is cold. In practice, you can hurry the process by placing the bird, still in its

plastic wrapper, in a large bowl or dish pan filled with cold water. Don't forget to remove the bag of giblets and neck which may be in the cavity of commercially frozen birds. *Never* cook a bird which has not completely thawed. There may be bacteria in the cavity which, if not destroyed during the cooking, can make you seriously ill.

If in doubt, just place your thumb in the cavity of the bird and forefinger on the outside and press. If it feels soft to the touch the bird is thawed – ice crystals would remain solid.

STUFFING AND TRUSSING

The purpose of trussing a chicken is to hold it in shape when it is cooked.

1. Turn the bird onto its breast and fold its wings behind its back.

2. Place some stuffing under the loose skin around the neck, then bring the skin down the back and hold it in place with a skewer, passing it from one side of the bird to the other through both wings.

3. Turn the bird on its back, place some stuffing in the cavity and sew up the skin.

4. Press down the legs and pass a skewer through them, and through the body, at the point where the thighs and drumsticks meet.

5. Tie the legs close together with string by looping it just above the knees, and draw the legs downward by making a final loop around the tail.

CUTTING UP

A chicken conveniently divides into 10 parts, but the two pieces of the back and the two wings will not make good servings on their own.

1. Cut off the outer sections of each wing at the last joint and the lower legs at the knee joints, and use these for stock.

2. Place the chicken on its back, pull one complete leg

away from the body then cut it off, feeling with the knife to find the thigh joint.
3. Divide the drumstick from the thigh, again at the joint.
4. Repeat for the other leg.
5. Cut off the remaining two sections of each wing where they join the body.
6. Separate the breast from the back by cutting through the rib bones on each side.
7. Divide the back into two by cutting across it.
8. Cut the breast into two by first dividing it at the neck end, cutting through the wishbone, then cutting downward alongside the breastbone.
9. To make more, but smaller, pieces, divide each breast, wing and thigh.

BONING A CHICKEN
Here are two methods of boning a chicken. Method B is a good deal more simple than A but it is less thorough, so for certain dishes you will need to use the more difficult method. For both you must use a very sharp knife, but be careful not to pierce the skin – apart from the initial cut in B.

Method A
1. Working from the neck end, loosen the skin from the flesh around the neck opening and cut out the wishbone.
2. Locate the shoulder joints on each side of the neck and sever.
3. Cut the flesh away from the bones in the first section of the wings and remove the bones.
4. Carefully extract the two outer wing bones – the wing tips can be cut off.
5. Start to work on the thighs. Loosen the skin and flesh so that you can cut through the top joint. Cut the flesh away from the thigh bones and break or cut the middle joint. Remove the thigh bones.

6. Work down the lower leg bones (drumsticks) and remove them. Leave the final pieces of leg beyond the drumsticks.

7. Cut away the flesh and skin around the central carcass. This must be done slowly and carefully in order not to break the skin. Pull out the carcass when it is loose.

Method B

1. Turn the chicken onto its breast, cut down the center line of the back, then work outwards and downwards, separating the flesh from the skeleton and taking out the thigh bones, wishbone and inner wing bones as you reach them.

2. Remove the whole central skeleton when it is loose.

CHICKEN CUTLETS

The method described below will give 2-4 cutlets from the breast and one from each drumstick or thigh.

Breast cutlets

Divide the breast in two, then separate the flesh from the breastbone and rib cage.

Scrape the meat gently away from the bones, making sure you do not tear it as you pull it off gently.

If they are large, each of the two cutlets can be cut in half to give a total of four cutlets from the breast.

Drumstick and thigh cutlets

Snap the joint at the bottom of the drumstick (just bend it back on itself) and cut through the tendons. With a small sharp knife, make a lengthwise slit down to the bone. Scrape the flesh away from the bone. Repeat with the other drumstick.

Use the same technique to remove the flesh from the thigh bones.

Basic cooking methods

BOILING

This is really a misnomer as the water should only be just simmering, or the flesh can become tough and dry. It is an ideal way of cooking a boiling fowl or stewing hen, as it tenderizes their otherwise tough flesh, yet keeps it moist. Put the bird into a pan, just cover with cold water and add 1 onion, a bay leaf, a sprig of fresh thyme or rosemary, 6 black peppercorns and 2 teaspoons salt. Bring just to the boil, lower the heat, cover and simmer gently for 35-40 minutes per pound. This is also a good way of cooking chickens that are to be served cold. Reduce the cooking time to 25 minutes per pound, then leave the bird in the water until cold.

ROASTING

Put into a roasting pan with hot fat, place in a preheated oven and baste regularly to keep the flesh moist and to get a crisp skin. Allow 15 minutes per pound plus 15 minutes (weight after stuffing) at 425°F, or 20 minutes per pound plus 15 minutes at 375-400°F. We give some variations to this procedure in our recipes.

To roast a stewing fowl, first simmer it gently (with the flavorings suggested above) for 2 hours. Leave until cold before stuffing it, then roast for the time appropriate to a roasting chicken of the same weight.

ROTISSERIE COOKING

This is a popular method of cooking poussins or small broiler-fryers. The birds can be split down the backbone and opened out flat. Roast for about 45 minutes at 400-425°F, basting frequently.

BROILING

Poussins, chicken halves or chicken parts can be broiled. Place the chicken 3-4 inches below a moderately hot broiler and cook for 8-15 minutes on each side, depending on size, turning them twice and basting with butter or oil occasionally.

FRYING

This method is used for chicken parts. Put the parts into a generous amount of hot oil or melted butter and fry until crisp and brown (about 10 minutes) on each side, then lower the heat and cook for a further 20 minutes, turning once.

BAKING IN A CASSEROLE

This is good for either a roasting chicken or a stewing fowl, but at least double the cooking time is needed for a stewing fowl.

Brown the chicken first to seal in the juices, then add vegetables and other ingredients and finally pour in the liquid. The casserole is then covered and either simmered gently on top of the stove for about 1¼ hours or cooked in an oven preheated to 350°F for about 1 hour. For chicken parts the time can be reduced to about 40 minutes.

MICROWAVE OVENS

We have not tried our recipes in a microwave oven, but if you are an experienced microwave user, or have a good cookbook, you might be able to adapt some of them.

A microwave oven can be a great help for rapidly thawing a frozen bird, or a cooked dish. As a rough guide, thaw a frozen bird for 6-7 minutes per pound on "full" power, 5 minutes resting, then 3-4 minutes per pound on "low" and another 5 minutes resting, or 6-7 minutes per pound on "medium," then 20-30 minutes resting. Some microwaves have special "defrost" settings, so check with your instruction book.

Carving

CARVING
Arm yourself with a sharp knife and a large fork so that you can hold the bird steady.
1. Leave a freshly cooked bird covered in a warm place for 10-15 minutes before carving it.
2. Remove any trussing skewers or string.
3. Take the end of one drumstick in your fingers, use it to move the whole leg away from the body and cut through the joint between the thigh and the body.
4. Cut the thigh and the drumstick apart at the joint and, if large, carve them into slices.
5. Cut off the wing on the same side, taking with it some of the adjoining breast.
6. Cut out the wishbone and surrounding flesh.
7. Cut downward slices from this side of the breast.
8. Carve the other side in the same way.

Preserving

FREEZING
To keep bought frozen chickens, simply put them, still frozen, in your own freezer. The recommended storage time for poussins, broiler-fryers and roasting chickens is three months. After this time a frozen chicken's bones may darken and there is said to be a slow deterioration in the flavor, but in our experience not a dramatic one, and we sometimes keep them much longer.

To freeze fresh chickens, choose young, plump, good-quality birds. Cover any protruding bones with foil, then put birds, individually, into freezerproof plastic bags or special freezer bags, excluding as much air as possible and sealing the bags tightly. Or wrap each bird tightly in freezer wrap, again excluding as much air as possible. Freeze the giblets separately. Wrap chicken parts in the same way. Keep utensils, hands and the birds clean.

Many of our dishes can be frozen and we have

marked the most suitable ones*. Some others, such as casseroles thickened at the end of the cooking with egg yolks, can be frozen before the yolks are added. These are marked* at the appropriate stage. Simply put the dish into a clean freezer container, cool overnight in the refrigerator, then place in the freezer. The dishes will keep for 2-3 months, but after this they *do* lose flavor. To thaw a casserole, leave it in the refrigerator overnight then place in a covered dish and reheat thoroughly – about 30 minutes at 350°F. Make sure there is enough liquid in the dish and stir it occasionally. If you froze the dish before completing the recipe, follow the instructions from then on.

OTHER METHODS

Nowadays, when all kinds of chickens can be bought all year round and kept for months in the freezer, the traditional methods for preserving chicken have virtually disappeared. However, chicken can be salted in brine to give an interesting, different flavor to the flesh.

SALTING IN BRINE

To make the brine, boil 3 cups coarse cooking salt, 1 cup brown sugar, 2 tablespoons saltpeter, 1 bay leaf, 1 sprig of fresh thyme, 5 black peppercorns and 5 juniper berries in 2 quarts water for 5 minutes. Strain the brine through cheesecloth into a plastic bucket or earthenware bowl and leave to cool. Place the chicken in the brine and keep it entirely submerged, if necessary with a weighted plate.

Stand the bucket or bowl in a cool place, and leave the chicken there for at least 2 days, and up to 3 weeks. The longer the chicken is left in the brine the more salt it will absorb. After two days it will need rinsing under cold running water. After 2 or 3 weeks it will need to stand in cold water for an hour.

Chickens preserved in brine can simply be roasted, when their special quality will be most obvious, or they can be used for most of our casseroles for an interesting variation.

Acknowledgments

We would like to thank all who have helped us. Some we mention for their particular suggestions. Others include Felicity Bettinson, Sheila Glossop, Charles Hodgson, Karen Robinson, Christopher Sales and Elisabeth Whipp. Our families have taken a keen interest and given much helpful advice.

RICH CHICKEN STOCK*

A good chicken stock is the basis of many of our sauces and most of our soups. Just boiling chicken bones and perhaps the skin may be enough for some purposes, but the recipe we give below produces the sort of strong-flavored stock that is essential for many dishes. Whenever possible, make stock before so that it can be cooled and the fat removed from the surface. Keep the stock in the refrigerator, reboiling it every other day or so. It can also be frozen – a useful standby when you haven't time to make fresh stock. This recipe yields about 7 cups.

bones and leftovers from a cooked chicken, or the raw carcass, giblets except the liver, and bones, of a boned chicken
1 large onion, quartered
1 carrot, cut in half
10 black peppercorns, crushed

2 bay leaves
salt

Preparation 5 minutes
Cooking 1 hour 15 minutes
Cooling 1½-2 hours

1. Put all the ingredients into a large saucepan, add 2 quarts water, bring to the boil, turn down the heat and simmer, covered, for at least 45 minutes, skimming off any scum that rises to the surface.
2. Strain through cheesecloth and leave until cold.
3. Remove the fat from the surface.

CLEAR CONSOMMÉ

This is how to turn chicken stock (opposite) into chicken consommé.

2 quarts chicken stock (opposite)
2 egg whites, lightly beaten
2 egg shells, crushed

Preparation 5 minutes
Cooking 1 hour 35 minutes

MENU PLANNING: Serve with Melba toast. Drink dry sherry.

1. Boil the stock in a large, uncovered saucepan for about 1 hour or until reduced by half.
2. Add the egg whites and shells to the stock and bring to a rolling boil.
3. Remove from the heat and leave to cool for 10 minutes.
4. Strain through cheesecloth.
5. Reheat and serve hot, or leave until cold and serve jellied.

COCK-A-LEEKIE*

This wonderfully rich old Scottish soup is really a main course. Some recipes suggest using a 2 lb piece of stewing beef as well as the chicken, but we usually make do with beef stock. If making the stock from cubes do not add any salt at the beginning and check the level before serving. The beef flavor goes excellently with the prunes.

6 lb boiling fowl
5 cups beef stock, made with 2 bouillon cubes if necessary
8 peppercorns, crushed
salt
8 leeks, cleaned
2 cups prunes, soaked for 6 hours and pitted
For the garnish
chopped fresh parsley

Preparation 10 minutes
Cooking 3 hours

MENU PLANNING: A main-course soup. Serve with a celery, beet and apple salad.

1. Put the chicken in a large saucepan, cover with the stock, add the peppercorns and salt, if necessary. Cover the pan and bring to the boil. Remove the scum from the surface.
2. Tie 2 of the leeks together and put into the boiling stock. Turn down the heat, cover and simmer for 2½ hours.
3. Chop the remaining leeks into 1 inch lengths and add to the stock, along with the prunes, either cut into halves or left whole, and simmer for 15 minutes.
4. Discard the leek bundle and remove the chicken. Allow it to cool slightly before taking off the skin and removing the flesh from the bones.
5. Roughly chop the flesh and return it to the soup. Reheat and sprinkle with chopped parsley.

HEARTY LENTIL SOUP

Do not serve this splendidly sustaining soup to start a meal because it *is* a meal. It makes a good supper – after an indulgent lunch.

¼ cup red lentils
½ cup rolled oats
5 cups chicken stock (see page 22)
1 cup chopped onions
2 cups peeled and sliced potatoes
⅔ cup light cream
1 cup diced cooked chicken

salt and black pepper
2 slices bacon, diced

Soaking 1 hour
Preparation 5 minutes
Cooking 1 hour 5 minutes

> MENU PLANNING: Eat with wholewheat bread and follow with a salad and cheese.

1. In a large saucepan, soak the lentils and the oats in the chicken stock for 1 hour.
2. Bring to the boil, turn down the heat and simmer, covered, for 30 minutes.
3. Add the onions and potatoes and simmer, covered, for 25 minutes.*
4. Stir in the cream and chicken and reheat but do not boil.
5. Taste for seasoning.
6. Meanwhile, fry the bacon until crisp and drain on paper towels.
7. Serve the soup with the bacon sprinkled on top.

CORN CHOWDER

For our version of a traditional New England chowder, half the corn should be "cream style," but if that is not available, use a 1 lb can of ordinary corn.

4 slices of bacon, diced
2 cups chopped onions
butter for frying, if
 necessary
3 cups chicken stock (see
 page 22)
2 cups diced potatoes
½ lb can corn kernels,
 drained
½ lb can creamed corn
2 cups diced cooked
 chicken
1 cup light cream
salt and black pepper
For the garnish
chopped parsley

Preparation 15 minutes
Cooking 30 minutes

MENU PLANNING: Serve with toast.
Drink a dry white wine.

1. In a large, heavy saucepan over medium heat, fry the bacon in its own fat until crisp, then remove with a slotted spoon and drain on paper towels. Crumble.
2. Fry the onions in the bacon fat, plus a little butter if necessary, for about 5 minutes or until soft.
3. Pour the stock into the pan with the onions, add the potatoes and simmer, covered, until the potatoes are cooked – about 15 minutes.
4. Add the corn, chicken, cream, salt and pepper and reheat but don't boil.
5. Sprinkle each serving with crumbled bacon and garnish with chopped parsley.

CREAMED CHICKEN SOUP

This is a good way to use the back, wings and neck of a chicken. Alternatively you can use ½ cup diced cooked chicken and 1 quart stock that has been made separately. Left-over creamed meat from Vallé d'Auge (see page 78) is particularly good and the resulting soup is really substantial.

wings, back, neck and, if available, bones of one chicken
6 black peppercorns
2 bay leaves
1 cup heavy cream
1 tablespoon plain yogurt
2 egg yolks
1 tablespoon butter
½ cup chopped onions
1-1½ cups diced boiled potatoes
salt and black pepper

Preparation 20 minutes
Cooking 2 hours

MENU PLANNING: A rich soup to precede a simple main course.

1. In a large, covered saucepan, simmer the wings, back, neck and bones with the peppercorns and bay leaves in 5 cups water for 1 hour.
2. Strain through cheesecloth.
3. Remove the meat from the bones and chop it finely.
4. Gradually blend the cream and yogurt into the egg yolks, then beat into 1 quart of the stock.
5. Melt the butter in a small skillet and fry the onions over moderate heat for about 5 minutes or until soft.
6. Add the potatoes, onions and chicken to the stock and heat through gently for 10-15 minutes, stirring constantly, but do not allow the soup to boil.
7. Taste for seasoning, and serve.

FEATHER FOWLIE*

An old Scottish soup. We use a little lemon juice to perk it up and serve the cream separately so that it can be added just before the soup is eaten. You really need a blender or food processor to make this dish.

6 lb boiling fowl
2 onions, roughly chopped
3 carrots, roughly chopped
1 turnip, roughly chopped
3 stalks of celery, roughly chopped
1 teaspoon dried mixed herbs
salt
12 black peppercorns
⅓ cup ground almonds
¾ cup fresh white breadcrumbs
juice from ½-1 lemon
For the garnish
chopped fresh parsley
For serving
⅔ cup heavy cream

Preparation 15 minutes
Cooking 3½ hours

> MENU PLANNING: Precede with a small glass of straight whiskey and follow with an egg dish.

1. Put the chicken, vegetables, mixed herbs, salt and peppercorns into a large saucepan, cover with cold water, bring to the boil, turn down the heat, and simmer, covered, for 2-2½ hours, removing any scum that forms.
2. Remove the chicken and allow to cool slightly before removing the skin and taking the meat from the bones.
3. Strain the stock through a sieve, and purée both the chicken meat and vegetables in a blender or food processor.
4. Return the chicken and vegetable purée to a large pan and stir in the ground almonds and breadcrumbs.
5. Gradually stir about 5 cups of the stock into the chicken. Return to the heat and simmer, uncovered, over low heat for 30 minutes, stirring occasionally.
6. Add lemon juice to taste.
7. Garnish with parsley and serve the cream separately.

VELOUTÉ DE VOLAILLE

A soup that specifically needs giblets for the basic stock, although you would never guess it from the delicate result. It must be eaten as soon as made, although the stock can be prepared in advance.

giblets from 2 chickens
2 carrots, roughly chopped
2 leeks, roughly chopped
1 stalk of celery, roughly chopped
1 onion, roughly chopped
1 clove of garlic
salt and black pepper

8 saffron strands
1 egg yolk
⅔ cup heavy cream
juice of 1 lemon

Preparation 15 minutes
Cooking 3½ hours, including cooling

MENU PLANNING: For a special dinner this can be followed by a rich main course.

1. Boil the giblets in a large covered saucepan with 2 quarts water for 15 minutes, skimming off the scum that rises to the surface.
2. Add the vegetables, garlic, salt, pepper and saffron to the boiling stock, turn down the heat and simmer, covered, for 1 hour, removing any further scum.
3. Strain the stock through cheesecloth, discard solids and leave the stock to cool until the fat can be removed from the surface – this will probably take a couple of hours.*
4. Reheat the stock.
5. Blend the egg yolk, cream and lemon juice in a serving tureen, then stir in the hot stock, a little at a time, until it is all mixed in smoothly. Serve at once.

SOPA PICADILLO

Chicken stock, ham, hard-cooked egg and fried croûtons are the usual ingredients for this peasant soup from Andalusia. The soup gets much of its flavor from the stock, so you must use a good one. The addition of chick peas makes it a meal in itself, and a leaf of fresh mint floating on each bowlful adds a perfect additional touch of flavor.

1 cup chick peas, soaked in cold water for 24 hours then drained
1 quart chicken stock (see page 22)
4 or 5 medium-thick slices of chorizo or other spicy sausage
3 tablespoons oil
8 slices white bread, crusts removed, cut into cubes

1 cup diced boiled ham
2 hard-cooked eggs, chopped
6 fresh mint leaves

Soaking 24 hours
Preparation 5 minutes
Cooking 1 hour 45 minutes

> MENU PLANNING: For a Spanish meal follow with Spanish omelet or our version of a Piperade (see page 75).

1. In a large, covered saucepan, simmer the chick peas in the stock for about 1 hour.
2. Add the chorizo or other sausage, and simmer, covered, for 30 minutes.*
3. Heat the oil in a skillet over moderate heat and fry the bread cubes, turning frequently, until evenly golden brown, about 5 minutes. Drain on paper towels.
4. Stir the ham and hard-cooked eggs into the chick peas and heat through, about 5-10 minutes.
5. Pour into bowls, float a mint leaf on each serving, then sprinkle on the bread croûtons.

CHICKEN AND PARSNIP SOUP*

We invented this soup when all we had left one Sunday evening were some parsnips and the remains of the chicken we had had for lunch. It could also be made from 1 cup diced cooked chicken and 3¾ cups stock that has been made separately.

the remains of a cooked whole chicken and the giblets and skin, if available
2 tablespoons butter
6 cups diced parsnips
1 teaspoon brown sugar
salt and black pepper

Preparation 20 minutes
Cooking 1 hour

MENU PLANNING: Makes a simple first course, followed by a light dish.

1. Take the meat off the chicken bones and simmer the bones with the skin and giblets, if available, in a large, covered saucepan in just over 3¾ cups water for 45 minutes, removing any scum that rises.
2. Chop the chicken meat.
3. Melt the butter in a saucepan over low heat and stir in the parsnips, sugar and 2-3 tablespoons of water.
4. Cook gently for 10-15 minutes, adding a little more water if the parsnips start to stick or burn.
5. Stir in the stock, chicken meat, salt and pepper, bring to the boil, turn down the heat and simmer for 5 minutes.

CHICKEN YOGURT SOUP

A slightly different chicken-flavored soup that is worth making.

1 teaspoon cornstarch
1¼ cups plain yogurt
2½ cups chicken stock (see page 22)
3 egg yolks, lightly beaten
2 tablespoons ground almonds

salt and black pepper
1 tablespoon butter
1 tablespoon chopped fresh mint

Preparation 5 minutes
Cooking 20 minutes

MENU PLANNING: A delicate soup that goes well with dry sherry.

1. In a small saucepan, mix the cornstarch with 1 tablespoon water, then gradually stir in the yogurt.
2. Bring to the boil slowly, stirring all the time, then turn down the heat and simmer until thickened, about 10 minutes.
3. Bring the stock to the boil in a covered saucepan, remove from the heat and allow to cool slightly, about 15 minutes.
4. Blend a little of the stock with the egg yolks until they are the consistency of thin cream, then stir the "cream" into the stock.
5. Stir in the yogurt mixture, ground almonds, salt and pepper.
6. Heat the soup over a low heat, stirring all the time until it thickens. Do not boil or it will curdle.
7. Melt the butter in a small skillet over low heat, add the mint and heat for 5 minutes. Stir into the soup just before serving.

PÂTÉS & HORS D'OEUVRE

SIMPLE PÂTÉ

There are numerous chicken liver pâté recipes, but we think this is one of the simplest and best. For variety, four anchovies can be chopped in – but reduce the salt. Because the onion is almost raw the pâté should not be kept too long, but do keep it for a few hours before eating, to allow the flavors to mature.

1 pound chicken livers
4 anchovies (optional)
½ cup butter
2 cups very finely chopped onions
1 teaspoon grated nutmeg
1 teaspoon dry mustard
½ teaspoon ground cloves
2 tablespoons sherry
salt and black pepper

Preparation 5 minutes
Cooking 20 minutes
Cooling 2 hours

MENU PLANNING: Serve with white bread toast. Butter not needed.

1. Poach the chicken livers in a little water for 5 minutes, drain and then grind in a meat grinder or food processor to a smooth consistency, with the anchovies, if using.
2. Melt the butter in a small saucepan over low heat until it begins to bubble, add the onions and cook for 2 minutes.
3. Stir in the remaining ingredients and, when thoroughly mixed, transfer to a bowl and leave until cold.

CHICKEN LIVER PÂTÉ

This is another simple chicken liver pâté that needs little cooking. It differs from the previous one chiefly in not using onions.

4 tablespoons butter
1 pound chicken livers
3 tablespoons sherry
3 tablespoons brandy
½ teaspoon dried thyme
½ teaspoon dried basil
½ teaspoon dried marjoram
1 clove of garlic, crushed
salt and black pepper

Preparation none
Cooking 18 minutes

MENU PLANNING: Serve with wholewheat bread. Drink white wine.

1. Melt the butter in a skillet, add the livers and cook over low heat for about 5 minutes – they should remain red inside.
2. Either mash the livers in the pan with the sherry and brandy, then thoroughly mix in the remaining ingredients, or mix them until smooth in a blender or food processor.
3. Transfer the pâté to one or more bowls and leave to cool. If keeping for more than a day, cover with a thin layer of melted butter to keep it from drying out and losing flavor.

TERRINE MAISON

For this you need a 1½-quart terrine (or casserole) which can be sealed with flour and water paste, i.e. one which has an inner rim on which the lid rests. You will also need a plate that will fit inside the terrine for pressing the pâté once it has been cooked.

8-10 slices of bacon
12 ounces chicken livers
1 small onion
12 ounces pork sausage meat
2 cloves of garlic
2 hard-cooked eggs, chopped
1 teaspoon each of fresh chopped thyme, parsley and basil (or ½ teaspoon of each dried herb)
salt and black pepper
2 chicken breasts, boned, cooked and sliced
½ cup flour

Preparation 20 minutes
Cooking 1 hour 30 minutes
Temperature 350°F
Pressing 12 hours

MENU PLANNING: Serve with pickles and relishes.

1. Line the terrine with the bacon.
2. Grind the livers, onion, sausage meat and garlic in a meat grinder or food processor until a stiff purée.
3. Thoroughly mix in the hard-cooked eggs, herbs, salt and pepper.
4. Place a thin layer of this mixture in the bottom of the terrine followed by a layer of sliced chicken.
5. Continue adding alternate layers, ending with the liver mixture.
6. Mix the flour to a stiff paste with about 2 tablespoons of water. Seal the terrine by placing a layer of this mixture around the inner rim and pressing the lid firmly onto it.
7. Place the terrine in a roasting pan of hot water and bake for 1½ hours at 350°F.
8. Remove the lid by cutting the hardened flour paste with a sharp knife. Place a plate over the top of the terrine, and put a 2-pound weight on the plate to press the terrine. Leave in the refrigerator for 12 hours.
9. Remove the weight and plate and invert the terrine onto a serving plate. It should slip out easily, but if it doesn't, hold the plate and terrine firmly together and give a sharp shake.

CHOPPED LIVER

The essential ingredient of this traditional Jewish chicken liver pâté is rendered chicken fat. No other fat will do.

4 tablespoons chicken fat
1 pound chicken livers, sliced
3 hard-cooked eggs
2 cups finely chopped onions
salt

Preparation 10 minutes
Cooking 20 minutes
Cooling 2 hours

MENU PLANNING: Serve with rye bread or matzo.

1. Heat 2 tablespoons chicken fat in a skillet, add the livers and fry over a low heat for about 4 minutes – the livers should remain pink inside.
2. Grind the livers to a smooth paste with 1½ hard-cooked eggs in a meat grinder or food processor until smooth.
3. Fry the onion in the remaining fat in a skillet over a moderate heat until soft and slightly colored, about 5 minutes.
4. Mix the onion with the liver, add the salt and transfer to a dish to cool.
5. Separate and chop the yolks and whites of the remaining hard-cooked eggs. Decorate the edge of the pâté with the white, the center with the yolk.

PÂTÉ-TERRINE DE VOLAILLE

An oval 1½-quart terrine is in theory best for this dish, but in practice the boned chicken can be made to fit tightly enough into a round casserole. The brandy is *not* optional, though it need not be a distinguished one and Grappa or Marc are legitimate substitutes.

chicken's liver and heart, finely chopped
8 ounces ground veal
8 ounces ground pork
2 slices of stale white bread soaked in ¼ cup milk
8 juniper berries, crushed
2 cloves of garlic, crushed
salt and black pepper
3-3½ lb broiler-fryer, boned (see method B on page 15)
8 ounces boiled ham, thinly sliced
8 ounces lean veal, thinly sliced
4 thin slices of bacon
2 bay leaves
2 sprigs of fresh thyme or 1 teaspoon dried thyme
⅔ cup brandy
½ cup flour

Preparation 1 hour 30 minutes
Cooking 2 hours 30 minutes
Temperature 300°F
Cooling 3 hours

MENU PLANNING: Serve with toast.

1. Mix the chicken's liver and and heart with the ground veal, pork, bread and milk, juniper berries, garlic and salt and pepper.
2. Place a layer of this mixture over the exposed flesh of the chicken, pushing it well into the spaces left by the thigh bones.
3. Cover with layers of ham and sliced veal, then add more of the stuffing mixture and continue in this way until all are used.
4. Reassemble the chicken and sew it up along its back.
5. Line the bottom of the terrine with 2 slices of bacon, then add a bay leaf and a sprig of thyme and place the chicken on top.
6. Pour over the brandy and enough water to fill the spaces between the chicken and the sides of the terrine.
7. Top with the other bay leaf and sprig of thyme and the remaining bacon.

8. Mix the flour to a stiff paste with about 2 tablespoons water and use to seal the terrine, as described in the recipe for Terrine Maison (see page 34). Bake for 2½ hours at 300°F. Leave until cold before opening.

CROSTINI

This Tuscan speciality is usually served before the main course. We have often eaten crostini in Italy, but frankly have never tasted any better than the ones we make at home.

6-8 tablespoons butter
½ cup diced ham
8 ounces chicken livers, chopped
1 tablespoon flour
½ teaspoon lemon juice
2 tablespoons chicken stock (see page 22)
salt and black pepper
10-12 slices of French bread

Preparation 5 minutes
Cooking 20 minutes

MENU PLANNING: No accompaniment needed except Tuscan red wine, say Chianti.

1. Melt 1 tablespoon butter in a medium-sized saucepan, add the ham and fry over low heat for 2 minutes.
2. Coat the livers in flour, add to the pan and cook over a low heat for 3-4 minutes. Pour in the lemon juice and stock and add the seasoning. Cover and cook for a further 10 minutes.
3. Meanwhile, melt the remaining butter in a skillet and fry the bread until brown and crisp, about 5-10 minutes.
4. Spread the hot chicken liver mixture on the fried bread and serve.

CURRIED FRITOS

To make these small Spanish treats look really elegant, make the stuffing quite stiff and deep fry them. Otherwise use plenty of hot fat in a shallow skillet. The filling can be prepared in advance.

For the filling
oil
2 cups finely chopped onions
2 teaspoons curry powder
3 tomatoes, peeled and chopped
⅓ cup chicken stock (see page 22)
salt
1½-2 cups ground cooked chicken
oil for frying

For the batter
1 cup flour
1 tablespoon oil
¾ cup chicken stock (see page 22)
salt and white pepper
2 egg whites, beaten until stiff

Preparation 30 minutes
Cooling and chilling at least 1½ hours
Cooking 15 minutes

MENU PLANNING: Serve on their own. Drink a dry white wine. Spanish if possible.

1. For the filling, heat the oil in a skillet, add the onions and cook until soft, about 5-7 minutes.
2. Stir in the curry powder, tomatoes, stock and salt and simmer uncovered over low heat until reduced to a thick purée, about 10-15 minutes.
3. Stir in the chicken. Leave until cold, then spread out on a plate and leave in the refrigerator to chill thoroughly. Make into small, walnut-sized balls.
4. For the batter, blend the flour and oil together, then stir in the stock, salt and pepper. Fold in the beaten egg whites.
5. Coat the chicken balls with the batter. Lower a few balls at a time into oil heated to 360°F and cook for about 5 minutes until evenly browned and crisp. Remove from the oil and drain on paper towels. Continue in this way until all the balls have been cooked. Check the temperature of the oil occasionally.
6. Serve hot.

CREAM CHEESE MOUSSE

Our friend Ruby Coghlan invented this featherlight chicken mousse. A blender or food processor is needed to get the smooth texture.

For the marinade
½ cup dry white wine
white pepper

4 chicken thighs, about 4-6 ounces each
8 ounces cream cheese
4 tablespoons mayonnaise
1 tablespoon gelatin dissolved in 3 tablespoons cold water
salt and black pepper

1 clove of garlic, crushed
1 tablespoon olive oil
1 sprig of fresh rosemary or ½ teaspoon dried rosemary
1 sprig of fresh thyme or ¼ teaspoon dried thyme

Marinating 24 hours
Preparation none
Cooking 40 minutes
Cooling 6 hours

MENU PLANNING: Serve with melba toast or crackers as an hors d'oeuvre, or with a salad for a light lunch.

1. Mix all the ingredients for the marinade together. Put the chicken thighs into a dish which they will just fit, pour the marinade over, cover and leave in the refrigerator for 24 hours, turning the thighs over occasionally.
2. Put the chicken in a medium-sized saucepan with the marinade and ⅓ cup water and simmer, covered, until tender – about 25 minutes.
3. Strain off and reserve the liquid. Remove the flesh from the bones and put into a blender or food processor with the reserved liquid, cream cheese and mayonnaise. Blend until smooth.
4. Add the dissolved gelatin to the chicken mixture. Blend briefly to mix. Taste and season, if necessary.
5. Pour into a shallow serving dish and chill before serving.

TERRINE WITH PORK*

You can grind pork yourself for this otherwise simple and tasty terrine, but it is a difficult business unless you have an electric grinder or food processor, so we usually buy ground pork.

1 pound ground pork
1¼ cups wine, red or white
8 ounces chicken livers, sliced
1 cup finely chopped onion
2 cloves of garlic, crushed
1 teaspoon fresh thyme or ½ teaspoon dried thyme
¼ teaspoon dry mustard

1 egg, lightly beaten
salt and black pepper
4 cloves
4 bay leaves
3 slices of bacon

Marinading 12 hours
Preparation 10 minutes
Cooking 1 hour 45 minutes
Temperature 300°F
Cooling 3 hours

MENU PLANNING: Serve with toast and fresh lettuce leaves.

1. Marinate the pork in the wine for 12 hours.
2. Gently poach the chicken livers in a little water in a small saucepan for about 3 minutes, then grind to a smooth paste in a meat grinder or food processor.
3. Drain the pork, reserving the marinade, and mix with the ground livers, onion, garlic, thyme, mustard, egg, seasoning and enough of the marinade to produce a moist, but not too soft, consistency.
4. Put into a 1-quart straight-sided ovenproof dish and top with the cloves and bay leaves, followed by the bacon.
5. Place the dish in a pan of hot water and bake, uncovered, in the oven for about 1½ hours at 300°F. The terrine is ready when it has shrunk from the sides of the dish.
6. Leave until cold, shake to loosen it on all sides, turn it out onto one hand, then reverse it onto a plate.

CHICKEN BEDSPRINGS

This was invented by Jessica, Cordelia's youngest sister, and consists of a combination of boned and lightly fried chicken, macaroni spirals and a strongly flavored herb sauce in which sage and rosemary predominate.

3 tablespoons olive oil
flesh from a 3½ lb broiler-fryer chicken, chopped into 1-1½ inch pieces
3 cups macaroni spirals
salt
oil

For the sauce
2 tablespoons tomato paste
6-8 tablespoons olive oil
1 clove of garlic, crushed
4-6 tablespoons finely chopped mixed fresh sage, rosemary, marjoram, thyme and chives

Preparation 30 minutes
Cooking 25 minutes

MENU PLANNING: Serve with celery baked with Parmesan cheese. Drink Chianti.

1. Heat the oil in a skillet and fry the chicken over moderate heat, turning once or twice, until tender – about 10 minutes.
2. Meanwhile, boil the macaroni in plenty of salted water, plus a few drops of oil to keep the pieces separate, until just tender – about 12-14 minutes.
3. For the sauce, simmer the tomato paste, oil, garlic and herbs together in a saucepan over low heat for 5 minutes.
4. Drain the macaroni, place in a warmed dish and put the chicken on top. Keep warm.
5. Add the cooking juices from the chicken to the sauce, reheat for 2-3 minutes and pour over the chicken and macaroni.

PILAU, CAPE STYLE

Our South African friend, Hansell Hewitt, introduced us to this pilau, which comes from *Cape Cookery: Simple Yet Distinctive,* published in 1890 by his great uncle, and which he claims was the first South African cookbook. Our version uses less than half the original amount of butter.

3-3½ lb broiler-fryer, cut into 12 pieces (see page 13)
the chicken's skin and giblets
1 onion, sliced
pinch of mace
1 clove
bunch of fresh parsley
salt and black pepper
⅔ cup milk
1 tablespoon flour
2 tablespoons butter

For the rice
1½ cups long-grain rice
2 tablespoons butter
1 teaspoon allspice
salt and black pepper

For the garnish
1 hard-cooked egg, chopped

Preparation 15 minutes
Stock 1 hour
Cooking 50 minutes

> MENU PLANNING: Serve with salad. Drink a dry red wine.

1. In a covered saucepan simmer the feet, neck, gizzard, heart, wing tips and skin of the chicken in 2½ cups water with the onion, mace, clove, parsley, salt and pepper for 1 hour.
2. Strain the stock, discard the solids, and return to the pan. Gradually blend the milk into the flour, then add to the stock.
3. Add the butter and chicken pieces, cover and simmer until tender – about 30 minutes.*
4. Remove the chicken pieces and keep warm.
5. Boil the liquid until reduced to a thick purée, about 10-15 minutes.
6. For the rice, melt the butter in a large saucepan, add the rice and cook, stirring, for about 3 minutes or until it becomes translucent, then stir in 3 cups water. Bring to the boil, cover and simmer for 12-14 minutes until the rice is just tender and the liquid is absorbed. Stir in the allspice, salt and pepper.
7. Make a bed of the rice on a warmed serving dish, put the chicken on top and pour the reduced stock over. Garnish with the hard-cooked egg.

CRISP AND SMOOTH

Once you get the hang of this quick and easy recipe it will only take about 15 minutes in all. The result is a delicious combination of tastes and textures.

1 tablespoon oil
8 ounces chicken livers, roughly chopped
1 lb bean sprouts
2-3 cloves of garlic, crushed

salt and black pepper

Preparation 5 minutes
Cooking 10 minutes

MENU PLANNING: Serve with a tomato salad. Drink dry red or white wine.

1. Heat the oil in a large skillet or a wok over high heat, add the livers and fry, stirring frequently, for 5 minutes.
2. Add the bean sprouts, stir well, then add the garlic and a generous amount of salt and pepper.
3. Cook for 4-5 minutes, then serve.

CANTONESE CHICKEN

This dish is as easy, and almost as quick, as the previous one.

2 tablespoons butter
1 tablespoon olive oil
2 medium-sized carrots, thinly sliced
1 green pepper, thinly sliced
2 cups bean sprouts

1½ cups diced raw chicken
2 tablespoons soy sauce
salt

Preparation 20 minutes
Cooking 10 minutes

MENU PLANNING: Serve with brown rice and scallions. Drink white wine or Chinese tea.

1. Heat the butter and oil in a heavy skillet or a wok over high heat, add the carrots and green pepper and fry, stirring frequently, for 2 minutes.
2. Add the bean sprouts, chicken and soy sauce and cook over a moderate heat for 5 minutes.
3. Taste for salt and serve at once.

CHICKEN LIVERS MADEIRA

Chicken livers make this an inexpensive, simple and effective dish.

4 tablespoons butter
1½ lbs chicken livers
2 tablespoons flour
½ cup finely chopped onion
2 cloves of garlic, crushed
1 tablespoon chopped fresh parsley

1 teaspoon lemon juice
1¼ cups chicken stock (see page 22)
salt and black pepper
½ cup Madeira

Preparation 15 minutes
Cooking 15 minutes

MENU PLANNING: Serve with mashed potatoes or boiled rice and baked tomatoes.
Drink Retsina, or a non-resinated dry white Greek wine.

1. Heat the butter in a skillet, add the livers and fry over a high heat for 4 minutes, stirring all the time to prevent burning.
2. Sprinkle in the flour and continue to cook over a high heat for 1-2 minutes until it browns.
3. Remove the livers and keep warm.
4. Add the onion, garlic, parsley and lemon juice, then gradually stir in the stock. Continue heating, stirring constantly, until it bubbles, turn down the heat and then simmer for 5 minutes.
5. Season, then stir in the Madeira.
6. Return the livers to the pan and reheat for 5 minutes.

PARMESAN CHICKEN

There are many different coatings for fried chicken, but we think lemon and Parmesan cheese is the most delicious. Use the chicken breast, cut into four pieces, the thighs and the drumsticks. The other parts can be used for a risotto (see pages 117, 120) or Paella (see page 89).

3-3½ lb broiler-fryer, cut up (see page 13)
½ cup flour
salt and black pepper
½-¾ cup fresh white breadcrumbs

2 tablespoons grated Parmesan cheese
zest of 1 lemon
1 egg, beaten
3 tablespoons oil

Preparation 20 minutes
Cooking 30 minutes

MENU PLANNING: Serve with broiled tomatoes and French fries.
Drink a light white wine.

1. Coat the chicken parts in the flour seasoned with salt and pepper.
2. Mix the breadcrumbs, cheese and lemon zest together.
3. Brush the chicken pieces with the beaten egg, then coat in the breadcrumb mixture.
4. Heat the oil in a large skillet, add the chicken and fry over moderate heat until tender – about 30 minutes. Wait until well browned before turning for the first time or the coating may become detached. Drain on paper towels before serving.

LEMON AND ORANGE CHICKEN

It's not as easy as you might think to give a roast chicken a lemon or orange flavor, but with the method we've devised the citrus flavor really gets into the chicken flesh. You can use an orange and a lemon, as we suggest, or you could use two of either.

1 orange
1 lemon
2 tablespoons butter, softened
3-3½ lb broiler-fryer
salt and pepper

Preparation 15 minutes
Cooking 1 hour 30 minutes
Temperature 350°F

MENU PLANNING: Serve with noodles and mushrooms. Drink a dry white wine.

1. Grate the zests from the orange and lemon and mix with the butter.
2. Squeeze the juice from the orange and lemon into a bowl.
3. Make a 1-2 inch slit in the skin of the chicken down the line of the breastbone, slip your fingers under the skin and ease it away from the breast. Insert the zest and butter mixture, forcing it well down on both sides. Pour in the juices.
4. Put the squeezed lemon and orange halves into the bird's cavity. Close with a skewer – there is no need to sew it.
5. Season the outside of the bird, then roast in covered roasting pan or wrapped in foil for 1½ hours at 350°F.
6. Skim the fat from the cooking juices and serve them as a sauce.

CHICKEN MARENGO

This is our own version of Chicken Marengo, the dish Napoleon's cook is supposed to have invented in northern Italy when the only things he could scrounge were farmyard chickens and wild mushrooms. Apricots are our addition.

4 tablespoons butter
3-3½ lb broiler-fryer, cut up (see page 13)
1¼ cups white wine
6 fresh tomatoes, skinned, or 1 lb can of tomatoes
1 cup fresh button mushrooms
2 cloves of garlic, crushed
1 chicken bouillon cube, crumbled
½ cup chopped dried apricots, optional
bouquet garni of a bay leaf, sprig of parsley and sprig of thyme
1 tablespoon flour

Preparation 15 minutes
Cooking 1 hour 15 minutes
Temperature 350°F

MENU PLANNING: Serve with potatoes boiled in their skins and a tomato and fennel salad.
Drink a dry white wine.

1. Melt the butter in a skillet and fry the chicken until browned, about 10 minutes on each side.
2. Transfer to an ovenproof casserole along with the frying juices and add all other ingredients, except flour.
3. Cover and bake for 45 minutes at 350°F.
4. Gradually blend the flour with 1 tablespoon of the cooking liquid, then stir into the casserole and return to the oven for 15 minutes.

CHICKEN AND CRAB

Chicken and seafood make a surprisingly good combination: you can also use chopped shrimp for this recipe. The drumsticks can be prepared in advance and will taste even better if cooked over a wood fire or a barbecue.

1½ cups flaked crabmeat
3 tablespoons butter
juice and grated zest
* of ½ a lemon*
1 tablespoon chopped fresh
* parsley or 1½ teaspoons*
* dried parsley*
salt and black pepper

8 chicken drumsticks
For basting
5 tablespoons olive oil
juice of 1 lemon
1 clove of garlic, crushed

Preparation 20 minutes
Chilling 30 minutes
Cooking 20-30 minutes

MENU PLANNING: Serve with baked potatoes and cucumber and yogurt salad. Drink white wine.

1. Mash the crabmeat with the butter, lemon juice and zest, parsley, salt and pepper.
2. Lift the skin of the drumsticks and slice the flesh lengthways to make room for the crabmeat mixture.
3. Push the crab mixture under the skin of the drumsticks and into the slit in the flesh. Cover with the skin. Chill for at least 30 minutes.
4. Stir the olive oil, lemon juice and garlic together in a small bowl.
5. Broil or barbecue the drumsticks under or over moderate heat, basting frequently with the olive oil mixture, for 10-15 minutes on each side, cooking the stuffed side first.

WEST AFRICAN PEANUT STEW*

You can make this traditional West African stew as hot as you like by adding more or less cayenne. Use crunchy peanut butter, and try to find a brand to which sugar has *not* been added.

3 tablespoons oil
1 cup chopped onions
1 cup chopped green peppers
3-3½ lb broiler-fryer, cut up (see page 13)
1 cup crunchy peanut butter
½ cup chopped peanuts
1 tablespoon vinegar
2 tablespoons tomato paste

½ teaspoon cayenne
¼ teaspoon ground cumin
salt
approximately 2½ cups chicken stock (see page 22)

Preparation 15 minutes
Cooking 3 hours
Temperature 225°F

MENU PLANNING: Serve with baked sweet potatoes. Drink beer.

1. Heat the oil in a skillet, add the onions and green peppers and cook over moderate heat slowly until soft, about 5-7 minutes.
2. Transfer to an ovenproof casserole with a slotted spoon, then fry the chicken parts over moderate heat in the same pan until evenly browned, about 10 minutes on each side.
3. Add to the casserole with the remaining ingredients, pouring in just enough stock to almost cover them. Stir to distribute the peanut butter.
4. Cover and bake for 2½ hours at 225°F, or at the lowest temperature at which your oven functions efficiently.

NORMANDY CHICKEN

Apples and cream are common in Normandy. This casserole uses cream, apples, and the Norman apple brandy – Calvados. The cinnamon is our own addition.

3 tablespoons butter
3 tart apples, cored, peeled and chopped
1 teaspoon ground cinnamon
3-3½ lb broiler-fryer
⅔ cup light cream
2 tablespoons Calvados

salt and pepper

Preparation 10 minutes
Cooking 1 hour 30 minutes
Temperature 350°F

MENU PLANNING: Serve with baked potatoes. Drink hard cider.

1. Melt the butter in a skillet and fry the apples over low heat for about 10 minutes, sprinkling them with cinnamon as they cook. Remove with a slotted spoon.
2. Fry the chicken in the same pan over moderate heat until evenly browned, about 10-15 minutes on each side.
3. Put some of the apples into an ovenproof casserole, place the chicken on top, then pack the remaining apples around and pour on half the cream.
4. Cover and bake for 1 hour at 350°F, turning the chicken over half way through.
5. Transfer the chicken to a warmed serving plate. Stir the remaining cream and the Calvados into the apples, taste for seasoning and cook over low heat, stirring, for about 10 minutes. Serve as a sauce.

NAIROBI CURRY

We learned this simple curry from Salim Yakub, owner of a Nairobi garage, later a member of Kenya's legislative council. It needed to be simple because Salim and his friends would buy live chickens in the market on their way into the country and kill, pluck, skin and cook the birds at the picnic spot, refreshing themselves with large whiskies as they worked. Everything was cooked over a wood fire.

3-3½ lb broiler-fryer, skinned and cut up (see page 13)
chicken skin and giblets
1 cup chopped onions
½ cup chopped green pepper
4 dried red chilies

salt
1 teaspoon turmeric
½ teaspoon ground cloves
1 teaspoon ground ginger
2 tablespoons tomato paste

Preparation 15 minutes
Cooking 1 hour 45 minutes

MENU PLANNING: Serve with white rice. Drink well-watered whiskey or beer.

1. Simmer the chicken skin and giblets in just under 2½ cups water in a covered saucepan for 30 minutes.
2. Remove the skin and giblets, add the chicken parts, onions, green pepper, salt and chilies and cover and simmer for 30 minutes.
3. Add the turmeric, cloves, ginger and tomato paste and simmer, covered, for another 45 minutes.

SWEET AND SPICY CHICKEN

This is an easy way of achieving a sweet and spicy baked chicken. The cooking time may seem long but this is needed to reduce the sauce and allow it to coat and penetrate the meat.

3-3½ lb broiler-fryer, cut up (see page 13)
salt and black pepper
3 tablespoons oil
1 cup butter
3 tablespoons Worcestershire sauce
2 tablespoons tomato paste
1 teaspoon brown sugar or honey
2 teaspoons lemon juice or vinegar
1-3 dried chilies

Preparation 15 minutes
Cooking 1 hour 15 minutes
Temperature 350°F

MENU PLANNING: Serve with cornbread and a green salad. Drink beer.

1. Season the chicken with salt and pepper.
2. Heat the oil in a skillet, add the chicken parts and fry over moderate heat until lightly browned, about 10 minutes on each side.
3. Melt the butter in a small saucepan and stir in the remaining ingredients plus ⅔ cup water.
4. Put the chicken into an ovenproof casserole, pour the sauce over and bake, uncovered, for 45 minutes, basting occasionally, at 350°F.
5. Remove the chicken from the casserole. Skim some of the surface fat from the juices before serving them spooned over the chicken.

POLLO VERDE

This is a dish which really does seem to be made more delicious by its appearance. The sauce uses elements from two Italian sauces, *salsa verde* and *pesto genovese*, and is a brilliant green. Three cups of fresh herbs may seem a large amount but do not use less.

For the sauce
juice of 1 lemon
10 tablespoons olive oil
2 cloves of garlic
3 cups chopped fresh basil, marjoram, mint or parsley in the proportions you like
3 teaspoons capers
3 tablespoons grated Parmesan cheese

3-3½ lb broiler-fryer, cut up (see page 13)
olive oil
salt and black pepper

For serving
2 tablespoons pine nuts

Preparation 15 minutes
Cooking 45 minutes
Temperature 350°F

MENU PLANNING: Serve with zucchini and mashed potatoes or boiled noodles. Drink a white Italian wine.

1. For the sauce, mix all the ingredients together in a blender or food processor.
2. Rub the chicken with olive oil, sprinkle with salt and pepper, put in a large casserole, cover and bake for 45 minutes at 350°F.
3. Serve the individual chicken parts covered with some of the green sauce and sprinkled with pine nuts.

FARMHOUSE ROAST CHICKEN

A simple French way to roast chicken – but just right.

3-3½ lb broiler-fryer
4-5 slices of salt pork or bacon
2 tablespoons butter

Preparation 5 minutes
Cooking 1 hour 30 minutes
Temperature 375°F

MENU PLANNING: Serve with baked potatoes and parsnips. Drink Burgundy, or another red wine.

1. Cover the chicken with the pork or bacon, tying them in place if necessary.
2. Place in a Dutch oven with ⅔ cup water and 1 tablespoon of butter.
3. Roast for about 1¼ hours at 375°F, basting every 10 minutes.

4. Transfer the chicken to a warmed serving dish and keep warm. Discard the salt pork or bacon.
5. Pour off excess fat from the cooking liquid, add 1¼ cups water and boil, stirring to dislodge the sediment, until reduced by half. Serve as gravy.

MUSHROOM CASSEROLE

If you cook the mushrooms separately, as we suggest, they retain their own flavor and give distinction to this otherwise simple casserole.

3-3½ lb broiler-fryer, cut up (see page 13)
½ cup flour mixed with ½ teaspoon salt
3 tablespoons oil
3 tomatoes, peeled and chopped
⅔ cup dry white wine

1 tablespoon fresh thyme or 1 teaspoon dried thyme
2 tablespoons butter
8 ounces fresh mushrooms, chopped
2 cloves of garlic, crushed
salt and black pepper

Preparation 10 minutes
Cooking 45 minutes

MENU PLANNING: Serve with sautéed potatoes and braised celery.
Drink a dry white wine.

1. Coat the chicken parts in the salted flour.
2. Heat the oil in a skillet, add the chicken and cook over moderate heat until golden brown, about 10 minutes each side. Transfer to a casserole.
3. Add the tomatoes, wine and thyme, cover and simmer over low heat until tender – about 30 minutes. If there seems to be too much liquid, remove the lid and let it reduce slightly.*
4. Meanwhile, melt the butter in a small, heavy pan, add the mushrooms and garlic and cook gently over low heat for 2-3 minutes.
5. Stir the mushrooms and their cooking juices into the chicken. Taste for seasoning.

POUSSIN WITH SOUR CREAM

Any young chicken can be broiled but poussins are best because they need the least cooking. The delicate flavor of the sour cream sauce exactly complements and enhances the flavor of the chicken.

2 poussins or game hens, cut in half through the breast
olive oil
For the sauce
1¼ cups sour cream
1 egg yolk
salt and black pepper

Preparation 15 minutes
Cooking 35 minutes

MENU PLANNING: Serve with peas and sautéed mushrooms.
Drink a young light red wine, say Beaujolais.

1. Run a skewer through the wing and leg of each poussin half to keep it flat.
2. Rub the poussins with plenty of olive oil.
3. Place the poussins under a hot broiler and brown quickly for a couple of minutes on each side.
4. Turn the broiler to low and continue to cook for about 25 minutes, turning occasionally, until the flesh is tender.
5. For the sauce, blend the sour cream with the egg yolk, then cook in a double boiler or in a bowl placed over a pan of hot water, stirring constantly, until the sauce thickens slightly, about 5-10 minutes. Add the seasoning.
6. Serve with the sauce poured over the poussins.

SAUTÉ À LA PAYSANNE

This is a splendidly sustaining peasant casserole, ideal for a cold winter day.

½ cup butter
2 lbs potatoes, peeled and cut into ½-¾ inch cubes
3-3½ lb broiler-fryer, cut up (see page 13)
⅔ cup dry white wine
⅓ cup chicken stock (see page 22)

2 bay leaves
1 tablespoon chopped fresh parsley, or 1 teaspoon dried parsley
salt and black pepper

Preparation 15 minutes
Cooking 1 hour 10 minutes
Temperature 350°F

MENU PLANNING: Serve with steamed cabbage and leeks.
Drink a red wine.

1. Heat 2 tablespoons butter in a heavy pan, add the potatoes and cook over moderate heat for 2-3 minutes.
2. Fry the chicken in the remaining butter in a heavy ovenproof casserole over moderate heat until evenly browned, about 10 minutes on each side.
3. Add the potatoes to the chicken, cover and bake for 45 minutes at 350°F.
4. Remove the chicken and potatoes and keep warm on a serving dish.
5. Stir the remaining ingredients into the cooking juices and boil, uncovered, for about 10 minutes or until reduced by about one-third.
6. Remove the bay leaves, taste for seasoning, then pour the sauce over the chicken and potatoes.

CHICKEN FRICASSÉE

In this recipe the chicken can really be tasted as there are no spices, except a little pepper, and no garlic to mask its flavor.

2 tablespoons butter
2 tablespoons flour
3-3½ lb broiler-fryer, skinned and cut up (see page 13)
1 cup chopped onions
2 bay leaves
2 sprigs of fresh thyme or 1 teaspoon of dried thyme
2 stalks of fresh parsley or 1 teaspoon of dried parsley
salt and black pepper
8 ounces fresh mushrooms, sliced if necessary
2 egg yolks, beaten
1 teaspoon lemon juice

Preparation 5 minutes
Cooking 1 hour 25-30 minutes

> MENU PLANNING: Serve with boiled rice and green beans.
> Drink Chablis or a dry white Bordeaux.

1. Melt the butter in a large, heavy pan, then stir in the flour until smooth.
2. Slowly stir in 3 cups water and cook over low heat, stirring constantly, for 5-10 minutes or until it thickens.
3. Add the chicken parts, onions, bay leaves, thyme, parsley, salt and pepper, and simmer, covered, for 1 hour, stirring occasionally to make sure that the chicken cooks evenly.
4. Add the mushrooms and cook for 5 minutes.
5. Transfer the chicken parts to a warmed serving dish, place the onions and mushrooms around it and keep warm.
6. Strain the sauce through a sieve, return it to the pan and boil for about 15 minutes or until reduced by half.
7. Blend the egg yolks with a little of the sauce to make a thin cream, then stir the cream into the sauce. Cook over a low heat, stirring constantly, for 5-10 minutes or until the sauce thickens. Do not boil.
8. Add the lemon juice and reheat gently but do not boil. Pour some of the sauce over the chicken and serve the rest separately.

ADVENTUROUS DISHES

GALLINA EN PEPITORIA

This is based on a recipe from the Palace Hotel, Madrid. Marinating the hen, adding green olives and reducing the sauce in the way given are our own modifications. These quantities serve 6.

6 lb stewing fowl, skinned and cut up (see page 13)
1¼ cups dry white wine
2 tablespoons olive oil
1 onion, sliced
2 bay leaves
salt and black pepper
about 1¼ cups chicken stock (see page 22)
½ cup sliced almonds
1 teaspoon fresh thyme or ½ teaspoon dried thyme
4 cloves of garlic, crushed
6 green olives, pitted

For the garnish
2 tablespoons oil
½ cup fresh white breadcrumbs
1 tablespoon chopped fresh parsley or 1½ teaspoons dried parsley
1 hard-cooked egg, chopped

Marinating 3 hours
Preparation 15 minutes
Cooking 2 hours 30 minutes

MENU PLANNING: Serve with mashed potatoes and boiled baby turnips. Drink a robust red wine from Spain.

1. Marinate the chicken in the wine for at least 3 hours, turning the pieces over several times.
2. Drain the parts and pat them dry. Heat the oil in a large, heavy-based pan and fry the chicken over moderate heat until lightly browned, about 10 minutes on each side. Remove the chicken with a slotted spoon and keep warm.
3. Fry the onion in the same pan over moderate heat for about 5 minutes or until soft. Replace the chicken, add the bay leaves, salt and pepper, the marinade and enough stock to just cover.
4. Cover and simmer for 1½ hours.
5. Add the almonds, thyme, garlic and olives and a little more stock if necessary. Cover and cook until tender – about 30 minutes.*
6. Transfer to a warmed serving dish and keep warm.
7. Discard the bay leaves and boil the sauce for about 15 minutes or until reduced to about 1¼ cups.
8. For the garnish, heat the oil in a skillet, add the breadcrumbs and fry for about 5 minutes or until crisp. Drain well on paper towels.
9. Pour the sauce over the chicken and sprinkle on the breadcrumbs, parsley and hard-cooked egg.

MIZUTAKI

A tabletop cooker or oriental hotpot is useful for this Japanese dish, or you can finish cooking in the kitchen, then keep the dish warm over a candle heater on the table. A heavy and preferably short-handled pan is also necessary. Chicken Mizutaki should be eaten with chopsticks.

For the sauce
¼ cup rice wine or dry sherry
¼ cup soy sauce
3 tablespoons lemon juice

flesh from 3-3½ lb broiler-fryer cut into 1 inch pieces
skin and bones from the chicken
1 onion
8-12 scallions, diced
bunch of watercress, chopped
4 medium-sized carrots, cut into 1 inch pieces
4 ounces fresh mushrooms, cut into 1 inch pieces
1 green pepper, cut into 1 inch pieces

Preparation 40 minutes
Cooking 1 hour 40 minutes

> MENU PLANNING: Serve with bowls of boiled rice. Drink hot saki.

1. For the sauce, mix all the ingredients together and pour into a small bowl.
2. Simmer the chicken skin and bones in 1 quart water for 30 minutes.
3. Remove the skin and bones, add the chicken pieces and onion and simmer gently for 35 minutes.
4. Take to the table and place over a low heat.
5. Add the vegetables and heat for 5 minutes.
6. To eat chicken Mizutaki, take out pieces of chicken and vegetable, dip them in the sauce, then transfer them to your mouth or to a bed of cooked rice on your plate.
7. Finally, use the remaining sauce, cooking juices and vegetables to make a soup which can be eaten as the conclusion to the meal or kept for another occasion.

WATERZOOI

This recipe is simple except for the final mixing in of the egg yolks, which must be done with extreme care or the sauce will be like scrambled eggs.

3 tablespoons butter
3 carrots cut into thin strips 1½ inches long
3 stalks of celery, cut into thin strips 1½ inches long
1 onion cut into thin strips 1½ inches long
2-3 leeks cut into thin strips 1½ inches long
2½ lb broiling chicken, cut up (see page 13)
1¼ cups dry white wine or vermouth
2 cups chicken stock (see page 22)

½ teaspoon fresh tarragon or ¼ teaspoon dried tarragon
2 sprigs of fresh thyme or ½ teaspoon dried thyme
4 sprigs of fresh parsley or 1 tablespoon dried parsley
salt and black pepper
6 egg yolks
⅔ cup heavy cream
For the garnish
chopped parsley

Preparation 30 minutes
Cooking 1 hour 30 minutes

> MENU PLANNING: Serve with sautéed potatoes and more buttered leeks or carrots.
> Drink a light German wine.

1. Melt the butter in a large flameproof casserole, add the vegetables and cook over low heat for 10 minutes.
2. Push the vegetables to the sides of the casserole, put in the chicken and cook over low heat for 10 minutes.
3. Pour in the wine or vermouth and enough stock to cover the chicken. Add the herbs, salt and pepper, cover and simmer gently for 35 to 40 minutes.*
4. Pour off the cooking juices and boil in a separate saucepan for 10-15 minutes or until reduced to about ¾ cup.
5. Blend the egg yolks and cream together, then very gradually stir in the reduced juices. Pour over the chicken and vegetables and cook over low heat, stirring constantly, until the sauce becomes thick and creamy. Do not let it boil.
6. Sprinkle with parsley.

CINNAMON CHICKEN

This dish seems to have been in the family for years. Cinnamon sticks make it look exotic, but ground cinnamon works just as well. You can do more or less the same thing with the individual chicken parts wrapped in foil, but it is not easy to contain the wine.

3-3½ lb broiler-fryer, cut up (see page 13)
3 tablespoons oil
4 tomatoes, peeled and chopped
3 cloves of garlic, crushed
3 cinnamon sticks, roughly crumbled, or 2 teaspoons ground cinnamon
½ cup ripe olives, pitted
1 orange, cut into 6 or 8 slices
1 lemon, cut into 6 or 8 slices
⅔ cup dry white wine
salt and black pepper

Preparation 20 minutes
Cooking 1 hour
Temperature 375°F

MENU PLANNING: Serve with fried eggplant and yogurt.
Drink a red Greek wine, say Demestica.

1. Put the chicken parts into a heavy ovenproof casserole and pour 1 teaspoon oil over each part.
2. Place the tomatoes around the chicken. Scatter the garlic, cinnamon and olives over the chicken and place a slice of orange and a slice of lemon on each part.
3. Pour in the wine and season with salt and pepper.
4. Cover and bake for 1 hour at 375°F.

PERSIAN PILAF

A recipe that depends for its quality on the candied peel. In Persia, this would be sliced thinly from large pieces. These are available but they are not always easy to find so you may have to buy ready-chopped mixed peel.

2 tablespoons olive oil
3-3½ broiler-fryer, cut up (see page 13)
⅔ cup chicken stock (see page 22)
5-6 saffron strands
2 tablespoons butter
1 cup chopped carrots
1 medium-sized onion, thinly sliced
¾ cup sliced almonds
1 cup chopped candied peel, rinsed if necessary

salt and black pepper
For the rice
2 tablespoons oil
1½ cups long-grain rice
¼ cup seedless raisins
¼ cup sliced almonds
¼ teaspoon cinnamon or 1 stick crumbled

Preparation 20 minutes
Cooking 1 hour

MENU PLANNING: Serve with broccoli or cauliflower. Drink beer.

1. Heat the oil in a heavy-based saucepan, add the chicken and cook over moderate heat until evenly browned, about 10 minutes on each side.
2. Add the stock and saffron, cover and simmer for 30 minutes.
3. Melt the butter in another pan, add the carrots and onion and cook over low heat for about 10 minutes.
4. Stir in the almonds and candied peel, then add everything to the pan with the chicken.
5. Season with salt and pepper and simmer for another 10 minutes.
6. For the rice, heat the oil in a large saucepan and fry

the rice until it becomes semi-translucent. Stir in 3 cups water, the raisins, almonds and cinnamon, cover and simmer until all the water is absorbed and the rice is just tender – about 12-14 minutes.

7. Serve on a large warmed dish with the chicken and its sauce in the center surrounded by the rice.

BLANQUETTE DE POULE

Veal is usually used for blanquettes, but chicken is just as good. Cut the bird into more pieces than you normally would; the breast into 5, the thighs and the drumsticks, if large enough, into 2, by cutting across the bone. Keep the back and wings for another dish – a paella perhaps (see page 89).

5 cups chicken stock (see page 22) or water
3-3½ lb broiler-fryer, skinned and cut up (see page 13)
12 small onions
6 cloves
1 carrot, chopped
2 bay leaves
2 teaspoons fresh thyme or 1 teaspoon dried thyme
salt and white pepper

4 ounces fresh button mushrooms
2½ tablespoons butter
2 tablespoons flour
⅓ cup heavy cream
2 egg yolks
4 teaspoons lemon juice
For garnish
chopped fresh parsley

Preparation 15 minutes
Cooking 1 hour 15 minutes

MENU PLANNING: Serve with new potatoes and buttered carrots. Drink a full-bodied white wine, say a Burgundy or Rhône.

1. Bring the stock or water to the boil, add the chicken pieces, cover and bring back to the boil.
2. Add the onions, one stuck with the cloves, the carrot, bay leaves, thyme, salt and pepper. Turn down the heat, cover and simmer, until the chicken is almost tender – about 30 minutes.
3. Add the mushrooms and simmer for 5 minutes.
4. Transfer the chicken and vegetables to a warmed serving dish and keep warm.
5. Blend the butter and flour together until smooth, then gradually blend in 2 cups of the strained stock. Return to the pan and bring to the boil, stirring, then turn down the heat and simmer gently for 20 minutes.*
6. Blend the cream and egg yolks together, then gradually stir in 5 tablespoons of the sauce.
7. Stir the egg yolk mixture into the sauce and cook over a low heat, stirring constantly, until the sauce thickens. Do not allow it to boil. Stir in the lemon juice.
8. Pour the sauce over the chicken and vegetables and sprinkle with parsley.

KAJU MURGH KARI

Although this is quite a hot curry it is not overpowering and the exciting tastes aren't lost. For a good curry it is essential to fry the onions and garlic gently and slowly. When finished, the curry should be thick and on the dry side.

3 tablespoons oil
2 large onions, chopped
3 cloves of garlic, crushed
1½ teaspoons fresh ginger root, finely grated
3 tablespoons curry powder
1 teaspoon chili powder
3 ripe tomatoes, peeled and chopped
2 tablespoons chopped fresh coriander or mint leaves
salt
3-3½ lb broiler-fryer, cut up (see page 13)
2 teaspoons garam masala
⅓ cup plain yogurt
1 cup finely chopped cashew nuts

Preparation 15 minutes
Cooking 1 hour 20 minutes

MENU PLANNING: Serve with boiled rice, chapatis, cucumber, yogurt and Indian relishes.
Drink beer.

1. Heat the oil in a large saucepan, add the onion, garlic and ginger and fry over low heat, stirring occasionally, until golden and soft, about 10 minutes.
2. Add the curry powder and chili powder and stir for 1 minute.
3. Add the tomatoes, herbs and salt and cook, uncovered, for about 15 minutes, or until reduced to a pulp.
4. Add the chicken parts and stir well to coat them thoroughly in the spicy mixture. Cover tightly and simmer gently until tender – about 45 minutes.
5. Stir in the garam masala, then gradually add the yogurt, stirring well after each addition. Simmer, uncovered, for 5 minutes.
6. Stir in the cashew nuts and heat through.

CHICKEN IN ALMOND SAUCE

A Spanish recipe which can be made with a broiler-fryer.

chicken giblets
3-3½ lb broiler-fryer, cut up (see page 13)
4 tablespoons butter
2 tablespoons olive oil
1 cup chopped onions
5 cloves of garlic, chopped
1 tablespoon chopped fresh parsley or 1½ teaspoons dried parsley
1 cup ground almonds
⅔ cup dry white wine
salt and black pepper
1 egg yolk

Preparation 15 minutes
Stock 30 minutes
Cooking 1 hour 30 minutes
Temperature 350°F

MENU PLANNING: Serve with boiled rice and stir-fried cabbage.
Drink a dry white Spanish wine.

1. Simmer giblets in 1¼ cups water in a covered saucepan for 20 minutes
2. Heat the butter and oil in a frying pan, add the onions and garlic and fry for about 5 minutes or until soft. Transfer to an ovenproof casserole with a slotted spoon.
3. Fry the chicken parts in the same pan over moderate heat for about 10 minutes on each side or until evenly browned. Transfer them to the casserole and add the parsley.
4. Strain the stock, discarding the giblets, and stir onto the ground almonds. Pour into the pan with the wine, stir well to dislodge the sediment, then pour into the casserole.
5. Add the seasoning. Cover and bake for 1 hour at 350°F.
6. Transfer the chicken parts to a warmed plate. Keep warm.
7. Blend a little of the liquid from the casserole with the egg yolk to make a thin "cream." Pour this back into the casserole, stirring. Place over a low heat and cook, stirring constantly, until the sauce thickens, but do not allow it to boil. Pour over the chicken.

CHICKEN PAPRIKA

Our version of this well-known dish comes from our Hungarian friend, Edith Corfield. Every Hungarian, she says, has his or her own recipe. Some versions use flour to thicken the sauce, but this is not necessary in our recipe.

3 tablespoons oil
1 cup finely chopped onions
1 heaping teaspoon paprika
½ teaspoon cayenne
1 clove of garlic, crushed
1 tomato, peeled and chopped
1 teaspoon tomato paste
½ cup chopped green pepper
black pepper
½ cup flour

salt
breast, thighs and drumsticks of a 3-3½ lb broiler-fryer
2 cups chicken stock (see page 22)
1 tablespoon sour cream

Preparation 15 minutes
Cooking 1 hour

> MENU PLANNING: Serve with boiled potatoes and broccoli.
> Drink a white wine, Hungarian if possible.

1. Heat half the oil in a large, heavy-based saucepan, add the onions and fry over moderate heat until golden brown, about 7-10 minutes.
2. Remove from the heat and stir in the paprika, cayenne, garlic, tomato, tomato paste, green pepper and black pepper.
3. Season the flour with salt, then coat the chicken pieces well. Heat the remaining oil in a skillet, add the chicken and cook over a moderately high heat for about 10 minutes or until an even light brown.
4. Add the chicken to the vegetables and pour in enough stock to just cover. Cover and simmer until tender – about 40 minutes.*
5. Transfer the chicken to a warmed serving dish and keep warm.
6. Boil the sauce for a few minutes to reduce it, if necessary, then stir in the sour cream. Pour over the chicken.

POLLO AL LATTE

Here is our version of this succulent Italian dish. Do not use more milk than we suggest, or it will take much longer to reduce the sauce to the right thickness. Other meats, such as pork and lamb, can be cooked by the same method.

chicken's liver and skin
6 slices bacon, diced
3-3½ lb broiler-fryer, skinned and cut up (see page 13)
1 onion, chopped
2 cups milk

3 cloves of garlic, chopped
1 teaspoon fennel seeds or dill seeds
salt

Preparation 15 minutes
Cooking 1 hour 20 minutes

MENU PLANNING: Serve with steamed potatoes and zucchini tossed in butter. Drink a dry white Italian wine.

1. Finely chop the chicken liver. Chop the chicken skin.
2. In a large, heavy-based saucepan, over moderate heat, fry the chicken skin and bacon in their own fat for 2-3 minutes.
3. Add the chicken parts and fry over moderate heat for about 10 minutes or until lightly browned on one side.
4. Add the onion, turn the chicken parts over and fry on the other side for 10 minutes or until lightly browned.
5. Add the milk, turn the heat to low, cover and simmer for 25 minutes.
6. Add the garlic and fennel seeds or dill seeds, turn the chicken over and simmer for another 25 minutes.
7. Remove the chicken and keep warm.
8. Add the chopped chicken liver to the milk and simmer for 15 minutes, or until reduced to a thick sauce, stirring frequently to free all the delicious cooking crust.
9. Taste for seasoning, then pour over the chicken.

CELESTIAL CHICKEN

An earthenware chicken mold is best for this dish, or use a casserole with a tight-fitting lid. The stuffing liquifies during the cooking and can be spooned out or poured into a bowl and served as a sauce.

8 ounces cream cheese or cottage cheese
1 teaspoon fennel seeds or 1½ tablespoons chopped fennel leaves
3-3½ lb broiler-fryer
salt and black pepper
⅔ cup dry white wine

2 tablespoons oil
4 leeks, chopped
4 carrots, chopped
4 stalks of celery, chopped
2 tablespoons brandy

Preparation 15 minutes
Cooking 1 hour 20 minutes
Temperature 400°F, then 375°F

MENU PLANNING: Serve with noodles.
Drink a dry white wine.

1. Mix the cream cheese and fennel seeds or leaves together, put inside the chicken and sew up the cavity opening.
2. Put the chicken in the bottom half of a chicken mold, sprinkle with salt and pepper and bake, uncovered, for 20 minutes at 400°F.
3. Mix the wine with the oil and pour over the chicken. Surround the bird with the vegetables, cover and bake for 1 hour at 375°F.
4. Remove the lid. Heat the brandy in a ladle or large spoon over a naked flame until it ignites, then pour, still flaming, over the chicken. Serve from the mold or casserole.

MANDARIN VELVET

A delicate and comparatively simple Chinese dish. The large amount of cornstarch produces a slightly gelatinous texture. Other vegetables, for example bean sprouts, can be substituted for the peas and mushrooms.

6 tablespoons cornstarch
2 egg whites, lightly beaten
3-3½ lb broiler-fryer, skinned, flesh cut into ¾ inch pieces
½ lb shelled fresh or frozen peas
4 ounces fresh mushrooms
2 tablespoons soy sauce
salt and black pepper

Preparation 30 minutes
Cooking 40 minutes

MENU PLANNING: Serve with rice and stir-fried mixed vegetables: zucchini, broccoli, bamboo shoots and carrots. Drink rice wine.

1. Mix 3 tablespoons of cornstarch with the egg whites and ¼ cup cold water.
2. Add the chicken pieces and leave for 15 minutes.
3. Bring a large saucepan filled with water to the boil. Add a few chicken pieces at a time and cook for 3 minutes.
4. Remove the chicken with a slotted spoon and rinse in cold water. Continue in this way until all the chicken has been cooked, making sure the water is boiling all the time.
5. Cook the peas and mushrooms in another pan in 1 cup boiling water for 2 minutes.
6. Add the chicken, turn down the heat, cover, and simmer for 8-10 minutes.
7. Mix the remaining cornstarch with any remaining cornstarch/egg white/water mixture, or if there is not enough, with a little cold water, then blend with the chicken and vegetables and continue to cook, stirring, for 5-10 minutes or until the sauce thickens.
8. Stir in the soy sauce and taste for seasoning.

PIPERADE WITH CHICKEN LIVERS

Chicken livers are an interesting addition to this well-known Basque recipe.

2 tablespoons olive oil
2 lbs green peppers, sliced fairly thickly
2 lbs tomatoes, peeled, quartered, seeds removed and juice drained
1 tablespoon butter
1 lb chicken livers, chopped
6 eggs
salt and black pepper

Preparation 15 minutes
Cooking 25 minutes

MENU PLANNING: Serve as a supper dish with hot buttered rolls. Drink a red wine.

1. In a large heavy pan heat the olive oil and gently cook the peppers over low heat until soft – about 15 minutes.
2. Add the tomato flesh and heat for 5 minutes or until it softens.
3. Meanwhile, melt the butter in another pan and cook the livers over low heat for 5 minutes, stirring occasionally – they should remain pink inside.
4. Beat the eggs, season generously and add to the peppers and tomatoes. Cook, over moderate heat, stirring gently, for about 5-10 minutes, until the mixture resembles soft scrambled eggs – it should not harden or the dish will be spoiled.
5. Stir in the livers and serve at once.

POLLO EN SALSA DE HUEVOS

Make the sauce for this Spanish dish in a double boiler or in a bowl over a pan of hot water.

3-3½ lb broiler-fryer, skinned and cut up (see page 13)
½ cup flour
4 tablespoons butter
⅓ cup white wine
⅔ cup chicken stock (see page 22)

salt and black pepper
2 eggs
2 tablespoons lemon juice
1 teaspoon dry mustard
½ teaspoon sugar

Preparation 10 minutes
Cooking 1 hour 10 minutes

MENU PLANNING: Serve with rice and spinach. Drink fruity Spanish white wine, say from Navarra.

1. Coat the chicken parts in flour. Melt the butter in a large saucepan over moderate heat and cook the chicken for about 10 minutes on each side or until evenly browned.
2. Stir in the wine, stock, salt and pepper, cover, turn down the heat and cook until tender – about 45 minutes.
3. Beat the eggs, lemon juice, mustard and sugar together and heat in a double boiler or in a bowl over a pan of hot water until they thicken, stirring constantly.
4. Stir in about ¼ cup of the chicken juices, then pour the sauce onto the chicken and cook over low heat for about 10 minutes, stirring, until the chicken is coated and the liquid almost simmers.

GALLINA EN PEBRE

This rich and succulent Spanish dish reverses the usual order of cooking because the chicken is first roasted, then simmered. To make it less rich, leave out the butter from the simmering liquid.

salt
3-3½ lb broiler-fryer
chicken's liver or 2 ounces chicken livers

1 teaspoon dried thyme or 2 teaspoons chopped fresh thyme
4 cloves of garlic

6 tablespoons butter
1 tablespoon olive oil
1 tablespoon lemon juice
⅔ cup stock (see page 22)
⅔ cup dry white wine
1 tablespoon chopped fresh parsley or a heaped teaspoon of dried parsley
2 bay leaves
1 egg yolk, beaten

Preparation 5 minutes
Cooking 1 hour 25 minutes
Temperature 400°F

MENU PLANNING: Serve with boiled rice and a green salad.
Drink a good red wine.

1. Sprinkle salt inside the chicken, then put the chicken liver and the thyme into the cavity.
2. Mash the garlic, half the butter, the oil, lemon juice and 1 teaspoon salt together, then spread over the chicken.
3. Roast for 30 minutes at 400°F, basting twice. The coating may turn black, but this does not matter.
4. Put the stock, wine, parsley, bay leaves and remaining butter into a large saucepan, add the chicken and the juices, cover and simmer for 45 minutes.
5. Transfer to a warmed serving dish and keep warm.
6. Strain the cooking liquid and return to the pan. Gradually blend a little with the egg yolk to make a thin "cream." Stir this back into the liquid and cook over a low heat, stirring constantly, until it thickens to make a sauce to serve with the chicken.

VALLÉ D'AUGE

This gloriously rich but quite simple dish is not for tender stomachs. We give it at its richest, but you can reduce the butter and use light cream.

4 tablespoons butter
3-3½ lb broiler-fryer, cut up (see page 13)
3 tablespoons Calvados
½ cup diced onion
1 tablespoon fresh chopped parsley or 1 teaspoon dried parsley
sprig of fresh thyme or ¼ teaspoon dried thyme
salt and black pepper
6 tablespoons hard cider
6 tablespoons heavy cream

Preparation 10 minutes
Cooking 1 hour 10 minutes

MENU PLANNING: Serve with plain boiled potatoes and boiled onions.
Drink hard cider or dry white wine.

1. Melt the butter in a heavy-based saucepan over moderate heat, add the chicken parts and cook for about 10 minutes on each side or until evenly browned.
2. Heat the Calvados in a ladle over a naked flame until it ignites, then pour over the chicken. Don't be alarmed by the flame the liquor will produce.
3. Add the onion, parsley, thyme, salt, pepper and cider, cover, turn down the heat and simmer until tender – about 45 minutes.
4. Transfer the chicken to a warmed serving dish.
5. Stir the cream into the pan and cook over low heat. When it just starts to bubble, pour over the chicken.

POLLO PISTO

For the best results use a fresh chicken. The chicken liver should be enough for the sauce, but you may have to buy 2 ounces chicken livers if the liver is very small.

3-3½ lb broiler-fryer, cut in half lengthwise
2 tablespoons butter
salt and pepper
1 tablespoon olive oil
juice of ½ a lemon
For the sauce
2 slices bacon, diced
1 small onion, finely chopped
2-3 large mushrooms, chopped

½ teaspoon flour
2 tablespoons Marsala, sweet Madeira or sherry
1 teaspoon brown sugar
¼ teaspoon ground nutmeg
salt
chicken's liver, or 2 ounces chicken livers, finely chopped

Preparation 10 minutes
Cooking 50 minutes

MENU PLANNING: Serve with rice and buttered leeks. Drink a red country wine.

1. Beat the chicken halves flat with a wooden mallet – the bones will break, but this does not matter.
2. Lightly butter a very large heavy pan (or 2 small ones) and add the chicken halves, cut-side down.
3. Melt the remaining butter in a small pan and pour over the chicken, season with salt and pepper, then cover each half with a weighted saucepan lid and cook over low heat for 35 minutes.
4. Turn the halves, sprinkle with olive oil and lemon juice and cook in the same way for 10 minutes.
5. For the sauce, fry the bacon over low heat in a small saucepan for 2 minutes. Add the remaining ingredients, except the liver, cover tightly and cook over low heat for 25 minutes.
6. Add the liver and simmer for another 5 minutes.
7. Divide the chicken into portions, place on a heated serving dish and pour the sauce over.

CHICKEN CHINOISE

This is a Chinese dish and needs one or two special ingredients, so perhaps you'll have to visit your local "Chinatown," although nowadays many supermarkets have Chinese shelves.

6 tablespoons butter
1 small onion, chopped
1 tablespoon oil
3-3½ lb broiler-fryer, cut up (see page 13)
4 tablespoons flour
1¼ cups chicken stock (see page 22)
1¼ cups rice wine or sherry
1 tablespoon yellow bean sauce
5 pieces ginger preserved in syrup, thinly sliced
2 tablespoons syrup from the ginger
8 ounce can water chestnuts, drained
salt

Preparation 15 minutes
Cooking 1 hour 30 minutes
Temperature 350°F

MENU PLANNING: Serve with rice or noodles and mangetout peas. Drink rice wine.

1. Heat 2 tablespoons butter in a large saucepan, add the onion and cook over moderate heat for about 5 minutes or until soft. Transfer to an ovenproof casserole with a slotted spoon. Add the oil to the pan.
2. Coat the chicken in 2 tablespoons flour and fry in the pan over moderate heat for about 10 minutes each side or until golden brown, then transfer to the casserole.
3. Melt the remaining butter in the pan, stir in the remaining flour, then gradually stir in the chicken stock and rice wine or sherry. Bring to the boil, stirring, and cook for 5-10 minutes or until the sauce thickens.
4. Add the yellow bean sauce, ginger and ginger syrup. Pour over the chicken, cover and bake for 1 hour at 350°F.
5. Add the water chestnuts, taste for salt and return to the oven for 5 minutes.

ORIENTAL GRILLED WINGS

The spices can be varied according to what you have but the ones we suggest make a successful combination. Putting them all in a blender with the oil and vinegar mixes them thoroughly, but they can equally well just be stirred together. These quantities will serve 6.

For the marinade
3 teaspoons ground coriander
2 teaspoons ground cumin
2 teaspoons ground cinnamon
1 teaspoon ground cardamom
½ teaspoon ground cloves
½ teaspoon cayenne
3 tablespoons white wine vinegar
2 tablespoons olive oil
1 tablespoon tomato paste
salt
1 onion, finely chopped

3 lb chicken wings, tips removed and the joints cut in half

Preparation 15 minutes
Marinating 4-12 hours
Cooking 10 minutes

MENU PLANNING: Serve with wholewheat bread and bowls of mixed salad. Drink a light red wine.

1. Mix all the ingredients for the marinade in a blender or stir them together.
2. Pour over the chicken and turn the pieces until they are all thoroughly coated.
3. Leave in a cool place overnight, or for at least 4 hours.
4. Broil for 5-7 minutes on each side.

CHICKEN CHEESE BALLS

This combination of chicken and cheese is unusually tasty. The chicken balls also look intriguing and it can be quite a surprise to cut into one. You can use any cheese, although we like a strong one such as Danish Blue.

6 tablespoons butter
5 ounces Danish Blue
 cheese, grated or
 crumbled
2 cloves of garlic, crushed
3½ lb broiler-fryer, flesh
 removed and ground
2 eggs

salt and black pepper
½ cup dry breadcrumbs
oil for deep frying

Preparation 30 minutes
Chilling 40 minutes
Cooking 15-20 minutes

MENU PLANNING: Serve on a bed of mashed potatoes with zucchini. Drink a dry white wine, Italian if available.

1. Mash the butter, cheese and garlic together and divide into 12 walnut-sized pieces. Put into the refrigerator for at least 10 minutes to harden.
2. Mix the chicken with the eggs, salt and pepper.
3. Wrap the chicken mixture around the butter and cheese and roll into smooth balls.
4. Coat the chicken balls in breadcrumbs and chill for at least 30 minutes.
5. Heat the oil in a deep-fat fryer to 375°F, then fry the balls in batches for 5-7 minutes until golden and crisp. Drain on paper towels.

ELABORATE DISHES

WHITE CLOUD

This Chinese roast takes its name from the shrimp chips which are served with it, but even more impressive is the deep chestnut color of the roast bird itself. The temperature is important. If roasted at more than 350°F, the skin may burn.

3-3½ lb broiler-fryer
salt
3 leeks, cut into 1 inch lengths
3 cloves of garlic, crushed
1½ tablespoons dark soy sauce
2 tablespoons dry sherry
1 teaspoon plain honey
For serving
shrimp chips

Preparation 25 minutes
Cooking 2 hours
Temperature 350°F

MENU PLANNING: Serve with fried rice with shrimp and stir-fried Chinese vegetables.
Drink hot rice wine.

1. Rub the bird with salt.
2. Mix the leeks with the garlic, and 1 teaspoon each of soy sauce and sherry. Place inside the chicken and sew it up.
3. Mix the remaining soy sauce and sherry with the honey and rub into the chicken. Leave for 15 minutes.
4. Put the chicken on its back in a small roasting pan or in the bottom half of an earthenware chicken mold (so that the cooking juices do not burn), pour the sauce over again and roast the chicken for 1¾ hours at 350°F. Turn it every 15 minutes, first onto its sides, then onto its breast, and baste it.
5. Divide the chicken into serving pieces, then reassemble into its original shape. Serve with the shrimp chips.

RIJSTTAFEL

This great dish from Indonesia, served with side dishes of nuts, fruit, vegetables and relishes, was brought to the West by Dutch traders. We give our version of the central chicken and rice dish.

*3-3½ lb broiler-fryer
1 lb onions (one small)
2 bay leaves
salt and black pepper
3 tablespoons oil
2 cups long-grain rice
2 tablespoons peanut butter
½ teaspoon chili powder
1 cup diced ham
1 teaspoon ground cumin
1½ teaspoons ground coriander
¼ teaspoon allspice
2 cloves of garlic, crushed
1 cup peeled boiled shrimp*
For the garnish
*1 hard-cooked egg, chopped
½ cucumber, chopped
½ sweet red pepper, chopped*

*Preparation 10 minutes
Cooking 2 hours*

> MENU PLANNING: Serve with small bowls of relishes, pickles, fresh tomatoes, cashew nuts, chopped bananas, grated coconut and raisins.
> Drink beer.

1. Place the chicken, the small onion, the bay leaves and salt and pepper in a large saucepan, add water to almost cover, bring to the boil, turn down the heat and simmer until the chicken is tender – about 1¼ hours.
2. Remove the chicken and leave to cool for about 30 minutes.
3. Heat half of the oil in another pan, add the rice and cook over low heat for about 5 minutes or until semi-transparent.
4. Stir in 3½ cups of the stock in which the chicken was cooked, bring to the boil, cover, turn down the heat and simmer until the liquid is absorbed and the rice is tender – about 12-14 minutes.
5. Finely chop the remaining onions and fry in a large skillet over low heat in the remaining oil for 5-7 minutes or until they start to brown.
6. Stir in the peanut butter and chili powder.
7. Skin the chicken, and chop the flesh finely.
8. Stir into the onions with the ham and the cooked rice and continue to heat until it starts to stick.
9. Stir in the spices, garlic and shrimp.
10. Transfer to a warmed serving dish and garnish with the hard-cooked egg, cucumber and red pepper.

MEXICAN CHICKEN

This Mexican dish may sound mushy, but is in fact delicious, the corn and chicken complementing the strong vegetable and olive flavors.

2 tablespoons butter
3-3½ lb broiler-fryer, cut up (see page 13)
2 cups chicken stock or water
2 cloves of garlic, crushed
salt
1 cup chopped onions
1 cup chopped green peppers
1 lb can of tomatoes, drained
2 fresh tomatoes, peeled and chopped
1 cup ripe olives, pitted
2 tablespoons flour
1½ lb can corn kernels, drained
4 slices of bacon

Preparation 25 minutes
Cooking 1 hour 15 minutes
Temperature 400°F

MENU PLANNING: Serve with boiled rice and squash. Drink beer or a white Californian wine.

1. Melt the butter in a heavy pan, add the chicken parts and fry over moderate heat for 10 minutes on each side or until evenly browned.
2. Transfer to an ovenproof casserole, add the stock or water, garlic and salt and simmer, covered, until the chicken is tender – about 30 minutes. Remove the chicken flesh from the bones.
3. Meanwhile, fry the onions and peppers in the heavy pan over a moderate heat for about 5 minutes or until they soften, then add the canned and fresh tomatoes and olives and cook for 5 minutes.
4. Stir in the flour, then gradually stir in about 1 cup of the stock in which the chicken was simmered. Bring to the boil, stirring, then turn down the heat and simmer for 2 minutes.
5. Place alternate layers of corn, chicken meat and vegetable sauce in an ovenproof casserole, beginning and ending with corn.
6. Top with the bacon and bake for 20 minutes at 400°F, then place under a preheated broiler for a few moments to crisp the bacon.

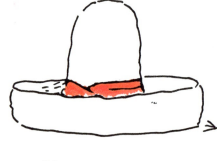

GOURMET HONGROISE

This Hungarian dish depends on the sauce (the chicken breasts and meatballs are bland in flavor).

For the sauce
2 tablespoons butter
1 onion, chopped
1½ cups chicken stock (see page 22)
½ teaspoon paprika
¼ teaspoon cayenne
black pepper
¾ cup heavy cream

For the meatballs
6 ounces ground chicken
6 ounces ground veal
¼ cup chopped onion
flour

For the lesco
1 tablespoon butter
½ cup chopped onion
1 cup chopped green peppers
4 tomatoes, peeled and chopped
salt

salt
4 chicken breasts
2 cloves of garlic, crushed
4 tablespoons butter

Preparation 35 minutes
Cooking 1 hour 50 minutes

MENU PLANNING: Serve with boiled noodles and zucchini.
Drink a Hungarian Riesling.

1. For the sauce, melt the butter in a heavy saucepan, add the onion and fry for about 5 minutes or until soft. Pour in the stock, season, cover and simmer for 10 minutes. Strain through cheesecloth, then boil for about 10 minutes or until reduced to 1 cup. Stir in the cream and reheat but do not boil.
2. For the meatballs, mix the chicken, veal and onion and form into 4 balls, using a little flour to make them easier to handle. Place in a covered steamer or colander over boiling water for 30 minutes.
3. For the *lesco* melt the butter in a skillet, add the onion and fry for about 5 minutes or until soft, then stir in the remaining ingredients and 1 tablespoon water. Cover and simmer until tender – about 30 minutes.
4. Sprinkle salt over the chicken breasts and rub in the garlic. Melt the butter in a skillet, add the chicken and cook over moderate heat for about 15 minutes, turning the breasts halfway through.
5. Place a chicken breast and a meatball side by side on each plate. Pour over the sauce, then top with *lesco*.

CHICKEN AND WATERCRESS

This is delicious either hot or cold. To serve cold, carve the chicken and put the pieces on a bed of greens, then pour the sauce into the center like a dip.

3-3½ lb broiler-fryer
1 onion, cut in half
1 carrot, cut in half
1 leek, cut in half
1 stalk of celery, cut in half
2 cloves
1 bay leaf
3 sprigs fresh parsley or
  1 teaspoon dried parsley
1 sprig fresh thyme or
  ¼ teaspoon dried thyme
8 black peppercorns, crushed
½ tablespoon coarse salt

For the sauce
2 tablespoons butter
1½ teaspoons flour
¼ cups chicken stock (from cooking the bird)
2 cups watercress leaves, finely chopped
⅔ cup heavy cream
2 teaspoons French mustard
2 teaspoons lemon juice
salt and black pepper

Preparation 10 minutes
Cooking 1 hour 30 minutes

> MENU PLANNING: Serve with new potatoes and mixed sautéed carrots and zucchini. Drink a dry white wine.

1. Put the chicken in a flameproof casserole and surround it with the vegetables, cloves, herbs and peppercorns. Sprinkle on the salt and pour in enough hot water to come halfway up the legs. Bring just to the boil quickly, removing any scum that rises. Cover, turn down the heat and simmer very gently for 1-1¼ hours until the chicken is tender.
2. Transfer the chicken to a warmed serving dish, cover and keep warm.
3. Strain the liquid, discarding the vegetables. Measure 1¼ cups and reheat in a small saucepan.
4. For the sauce, melt the butter in a saucepan, stir in the flour and cook over low heat for 1 minute, then gradually stir in the warm stock. Bring to the boil, stirring, then turn down the heat and simmer for 2 minutes. Cool for about 10 minutes.
5. Blend the watercress with the cream.
6. Stir the watercress and cream, mustard and lemon juice into the sauce and reheat, stirring – do not boil. Taste for seasoning, then pour over the chicken.

PAELLA

A paella can include any number of different kinds of meat and fish. The proportion of these to the rice can also vary. In Spain, if the dish is served as a first course, it often consists of little except rice. But if it is to be a main course, use at least the quantities we suggest. As for saffron, we give the amount usually recommended, but, heretical as it may sound, suggest adding a drop or two of yellow food coloring as well. Don't use turmeric as it will give a different flavor. These quantities will serve at least ten.

3 tablespoons olive oil
2 cups chopped onions
4 cloves of garlic, finely chopped
2 cups chopped red peppers
4 tomatoes, sliced
2 lb poussin, cut up, or 6 chicken wings
2 ounces hot chorizo, or other spicy, dry sausage, sliced
4 cups short-grain rice

10 saffron strands, soaked in a little milk
2 cups shelled or frozen peas
12 mussels in their shells
8 ounces other shellfish
salt and black pepper
10 large unpeeled shrimp

Preparation 10 minutes
Cooking 1 hour

MENU PLANNING: A complete meal which needs no accompaniments. Drink a Spanish white wine.

1. Heat the oil in a large pan, add the onions, garlic and half the peppers and fry over moderate heat for 5-10 minutes or until softened.
2. Add the tomatoes and continue to cook for 3-4 minutes, stirring occasionally.
3. Add the poussin or wings and chorizo and fry over moderate heat for about 15 minutes or until evenly browned, turning once or twice.
4. Add the rice and cook, stirring, for a few minutes or until translucent.
5. Stir in 2 quarts water, and the saffron and remaining peppers. Simmer, uncovered, for 15 minutes.
6. Add the peas, mussels and shellfish, stir again and taste for seasoning. Place the shrimp on top, cover and cook over low heat for about 15 minutes or until everything is thoroughly heated.

POULE AU POT HENRI IV

This economical and delicious French dish was named after the 16th-century king who wanted all his subjects to have a chicken in the pot every Sunday. These quantities will serve 6.

5 lb roasting chicken
For the stock
giblets (except the liver) and the wing tips of the chicken
small veal knuckle or piece of bacon
2 carrots, roughly chopped
2 small turnips, roughly chopped
2 onions, one of them stuck with 4 cloves
2 leeks, roughly chopped
1 stalk of celery, roughly chopped
1 bay leaf
sprig of fresh parsley
salt and black pepper

For the stuffing
5 slices stale white bread, crusts removed, soaked in 2/3 cup milk
chicken's liver
1 thick slice of ham, chopped
pinch of nutmeg
2 cloves of garlic, chopped
2 tablespoons chopped fresh parsley
salt and black pepper
2 eggs, beaten

Preparation 25 minutes
Cooking 2 hours 30 minutes
Cooling 2 hours

MENU PLANNING: Serve with buttered baked parsnips or turnips and cabbage. Drink an ordinary red wine, French if available.

1. For the stock, simmer all the ingredients in a large covered saucepan for 1 hour in 2½ quarts water, removing scum as it forms. Leave until cold, then remove the fat.
2. For the stuffing, mash the bread and milk and add the remaining ingredients, mixing in the eggs last.
3. Place the stuffing in the bird's cavity and under the flap of neck skin. Wrap the bird in a clean dish towel, tying it securely. This keeps the stuffing in place.
4. Strain the stock, discarding the solids, and bring to the boil in a large, heavy pan. Lower in the chicken, turn down the heat and simmer, covered, for 1½ hours. Do not overcook.
5. Remove from the stock. Serve the stock as a sauce.

POLISH PATTIES

These patties are messy to make because the beaten egg whites make the mixture hard to handle, but that is why they are so light. You will need a hot oven ready to bake them in when they have been fried.

For the sauce
3 hard-cooked egg yolks, finely mashed
2 teaspoons lemon juice
1 teaspoon sugar
4 teaspoons Dijon-style mustard
⅔ cup stock (see page 22)
3 teaspoons capers
For the chicken patties
6 tablespoons butter
½ cup chopped fresh mushrooms
3 eggs, 2 separated

2 slices of white bread with crusts removed, soaked in milk
2 boned chicken breasts, skinned and ground
salt and black pepper
½ cup dry breadcrumbs

Sauce 15 minutes
Preparation 30 minutes
Chilling 30 minutes
Cooking 30 minutes
Temperature 400°F

MENU PLANNING: Serve with spicy red cabbage cooked with caraway seeds, brown sugar and vinegar.
Drink a German white wine.

1. For the sauce, cream the egg yolks with the lemon juice, sugar and mustard, then gradually blend in the stock. Add the capers, cover and refrigerate.
2. For the chicken patties, melt 1 tablespoon butter in a skillet, add the mushrooms and cook over low heat for about 5 minutes or until softened.
3. Cream the 2 egg yolks with 1 tablespoon butter.
4. Squeeze the soaked bread, mash it, then add to the egg yolk and butter mixture. Mix in the cooked mushrooms, the ground chicken and salt and pepper.
5. Beat the 2 egg whites until stiff, then fold into the chicken mixture. Form into small patties and refrigerate for at least 30 minutes.
6. Mix the remaining egg with the breadcrumbs and use to coat the chicken patties.
7. Melt the remaining butter in a skillet over high heat, but do not let it burn. Fry the chicken patties for about 10-15 minutes or until golden brown all over. Arrange them on a cookie sheet and put them in a preheated oven at 400°F for 10 minutes.
10. Serve the patties and sauce separately.

BROILED CHICKEN MAINTENON

Louis XIV's chef named this dish after the king's mistress, the Marquise de Maintenon. For a really splendid result, use slices of homemade wholewheat bread for the toast. Because each serving sits on a slice of toast, the chicken should be quartered to make the right number of servings.

½ cup butter
juice of ½ a lemon
3-3½ lb broiler-fryer, quartered
1 cup sliced fresh mushrooms
1 cup chopped cooked tongue
2 chicken livers, chopped
¾ cup dry white wine or dry sherry
2 sprigs of fresh thyme or 1 teaspoon dried thyme
salt and black pepper
4 slices of wholewheat bread for toast

For the garnish
sprigs of parsley

Preparation 20 minutes
Cooking 35 minutes

MENU PLANNING: Serve with buttered green beans and braised celery. Drink a fine red wine.

1. Melt 4 tablespoons butter and mix with the lemon juice.
2. Broil the chicken quarters for 15-20 minutes, turning several times and basting occasionally with the butter/lemon juice mixture.
3. Melt 2 tablespoons butter in a skillet over low heat and cook the mushrooms and tongue together for 3-4 minutes, stirring occasionally. Drain the cooking juices and reserve.
4. Melt the remaining butter in a skillet over low heat and cook the chicken livers for about 5 minutes. Chop them finely and set aside.
5. Bring the wine to the boil in a small, covered saucepan, then add the chopped livers, thyme, salt, pepper and the cooking juices from the tongue and mushrooms and heat through gently.
6. Toast the bread.
7. Assemble each serving in the following order: toast at the bottom (buttered if you like), a layer of the tongue and mushroom mixture, a chicken quarter, then the liver and wine sauce. Garnish with parsley.

CHICKEN KIEV

This spectacular Russian dish is also well known in Italy as *"pollo sorpresa."* Make sure the chicken is sewn up tightly around its "surprise" butter filling and that each piece is dipped twice in the coating. Warn guests that the melted butter may spurt from the chicken when it is cut and that it will be hot.

½ cup butter
2 tablespoons chopped parsley
1 tablespoon grated lemon rind
1 tablespoon lemon juice
2 cloves of garlic, crushed
salt and black pepper

4 chicken breasts, skinned and boned (see page 14)
2 eggs, beaten
1½ cups fresh white breadcrumbs
oil for deep frying

Preparation 1 hour
Chilling 30 minutes
Cooking 6 minutes

MENU PLANNING: Serve with mashed potatoes and a lettuce and avocado salad. Drink a dry white wine.

1. Cream the butter with the parsley, lemon rind and juice, garlic and seasoning. Shape into a block and leave in the freezer for 30 minutes to harden.
2. Pound the chicken breasts flat. It is easier to do this between sheets of waxed paper.
3. Cut the butter into 4 long thin "fingers" and wrap each in a chicken breast. Sew up tightly with needle and thread.
4. Dip each breast in beaten egg, then coat well with breadcrumbs. Repeat once more.
5. Heat the oil to about 375°F in a deep-fat fryer and fry the chicken until golden brown. This will take 5-6 minutes. Drain on paper towels.
6. Remove the threads before serving.

SAUTÉ AUX OLIVES

This dish has the rich aroma and flavor that is so typical of the cooking from the south of France. Use fresh herbs if possible. The oil-cured ripe olives from France and Morocco are easily pitted and have the strong taste that this dish needs. They are available from delicatessens and gourmet food stores.

3 cloves of garlic
6 sprigs of fresh thyme and 1 sprig each of thyme, marjoram and basil
3-3½ lb broiler-fryer, cut up (see page 13)
juice of ½ a lemon
3 tablespoons olive oil
½ cup red or dry white wine
2 anchovies
4 tomatoes, chopped
1 cup oil-cured ripe pitted olives

Preparation 30 minutes
Cooking 1 hour

MENU PLANNING: Serve with baked potatoes and buttered peas. Drink a dry rosé wine.

1. Thinly slice 1 clove of garlic and insert a slice with a small sprig of thyme between the skin and flesh of each joint, then sprinkle the joints with lemon juice.
2. Heat the oil in a frying pan over low heat and fry the chicken parts, skin side first, for about 10 minutes each side or until evenly browned.
3. Cover and cook for 20 minutes, then transfer with most of the oil to an ovenproof casserole. Cover and place in an oven at the lowest temperature at which it will function efficiently while finishing the dish.
4. Stir the wine into the oil remaining in the pan and boil for about 5 minutes or until slightly syrupy.
5. Crush the anchovies with the remaining garlic and stir into the wine with a sprig each of thyme, marjoram and basil and the tomatoes.
6. Simmer over low heat for about 10 minutes or until the tomatoes are soft. Add the olives and heat for 3-4 minutes.
7. Place the chicken on a warmed serving dish and pour the sauce over.

CHICKEN PROVENÇAL

For this we use a classic rich sauce with red wine from the south of France.

1 tablespoon olive oil
2 tablespoons butter
3 medium onions, chopped
3 medium carrots, chopped
1 stalk of celery, chopped
2 slices of bacon, chopped
3 cloves of garlic, finely chopped
1 lb can of tomatoes
1 heaping teaspoon sugar
1 tablespoon white wine vinegar
⅔ cup red wine
salt and black pepper
1 tablespoon chopped fresh basil and parsley
3 tablespoons oil
3-3½ lb broiler-fryer
½ cup flour
2 cups fresh button mushrooms

Preparation 10 minutes
Cooking 1 hour 15 minutes

MENU PLANNING: Serve with new potatoes and spinach.
Drink a red wine.

1. Heat the oil and butter in a large flameproof casserole, add the onions, carrots, celery, bacon and garlic, cover and cook over a moderate heat for 10 minutes.
2. Remove the lid and turn the heat to high for about 5 minutes or until the vegetables start to brown.
3. Add the tomatoes, sugar, vinegar, wine, salt, pepper and herbs and simmer, covered, for 15 minutes.
4. Meanwhile, heat the oil in a skillet over moderate heat. Coat the chicken in flour, then fry the chicken in the oil for about 15 minutes or until evenly browned all over.
5. Add the chicken to the vegetables, cover the pan and simmer over low heat for 40 minutes.
6. Add the mushrooms and simmer, covered, for 5 minutes.

SENEGAL CHICKEN

When we discovered this recipe it opened up a new culinary world to us – cooking with fresh coconut.

12 black peppercorns, or 1 teaspoon ground black pepper
4 cloves, or ½ teaspoon ground cloves
½ teaspoon ground ginger
salt
3-3½ lb broiler-fryer, cut up (see page 13)

4 tablespoons oil
1¼ cups finely chopped onions
1 fresh coconut
2 tablespoons butter
1 teaspoon cayenne

Preparation 25 minutes
Cooking 1 hour

MENU PLANNING: Serve with boiled millet or cracked wheat and grilled tomatoes. Drink a dry red wine.

1. Grind the peppercorns and cloves, if necessary, and mix with the ginger and salt. Coat the chicken parts with this mixture.
2. Heat the oil in a large skillet, add the onions and cook over moderate heat for about 5 minutes or until soft.
3. Add the chicken parts and cook over low heat, turning frequently, for 40 minutes. Transfer the chicken to a warmed serving dish and keep warm.
4. Meanwhile, crack the coconut, reserve the "milk" (about ⅔ cup), cut out the flesh and grate it.
5. Melt the butter in a saucepan, add the grated coconut and cook, stirring occasionally, for 10-15 minutes, until softened and starting to turn golden.
6. Stir the coconut milk into the onions, bring to the boil, turn down the heat and simmer for 5 minutes, then season with salt and cayenne.
7. To serve, spoon the fried coconut over the chicken then pour the coconut milk and onion mixture over.

CHICKEN BÉARNAIS

This classic French recipe uses a stewing fowl. Make the sauce while the chicken is cooking. This dish serves 6.

For the stuffing
chicken's liver and heart
½ cup fresh white breadcrumbs
4 ounces sausage meat
1 egg
1 tablespoon chopped fresh parsley or 2 teaspoons dried parsley
2 teaspoons dried mixed herbs
salt and black pepper
⅔ cup milk
butter for frying
5-6 lb stewing fowl
1 onion, roughly chopped
2 carrots, roughly chopped
1 turnip, roughly chopped
1 stalk of celery
1 leek, roughly chopped

For the sauce
1 small onion, finely chopped
1 teaspoon finely chopped chives
1 teaspoon finely chopped parsley
3 tablespoons olive oil
1 teaspoon lemon juice
salt and black pepper
1 egg

Preparation 30 minutes
Cooking 3 hours 10 minutes

MENU PLANNING: Serve with additional vegetables that have been added to the chicken 20 minutes before the end of the cooking.
Drink a dry red wine.

1. For the stuffing, poach the liver and heart in a little water for 5 minutes, then grind finely in a meat grinder or food processor. Mix with the breadcrumbs, sausage meat, egg, herbs, salt and pepper and add enough milk to make it a stiff consistency. Stuff the bird and sew it up.
2. Melt the butter in a large, heavy-based saucepan, add the bird and cook over moderate heat for 15-20 minutes until evenly browned all over.
3. Just cover with water, add the vegetables, cover the pan and simmer gently for 3 hours.
4. For the sauce, stir the onion, chives and parsley into the olive oil and lemon juice and add salt and pepper.
5. Boil the egg for 3 minutes, then stir the half-cooked yolk and the mashed white into the sauce.
6. Serve the chicken sliced and accompanied by the sauce.

MOROCCAN CHICKEN

The salted lemons must be prepared a month in advance. The distinctive lemon and salt flavor makes it quite unlike any other chicken casserole.

For the salted lemons
1 cup salt
1 teaspoon peppercorns
1 teaspoon coriander seeds
3 lemons, each cut into 6 slices
juice of 1 lemon

MENU PLANNING: Serve with boiled rice and ratatouille.
Drink a full-bodied red wine.

1. Mix the salt, peppercorns and coriander seeds together and rub into the lemon slices.
2. Pack tightly into a glass jar.
3. Pour in the lemon juice, then cover the jar and keep in a cool place for at least a month. As slices are removed, more fresh slices can be added to the brine, pushing them well down into the jar. Use the slices in the order in which they have been salted. Top up the jar with lemon juice if necessary.

For the Moroccan chicken
3 tablespoons olive oil
4 chicken thighs with legs
1 cup chopped onions
1 cup chopped red peppers
1 clove of garlic, crushed
½ teaspoon ground ginger
¼ teaspoon ground cinnamon
4 slices salted lemon, rinsed
1½ lbs small new potatoes, peeled
¼ cup sliced almonds
¼ cup pitted ripe olives

Salting 1 month
Preparation 10 minutes
Cooking 1 hour

1. Heat the oil in a large, heavy-based pan, add the chicken and fry over moderate heat for about 10 minutes on each side or until evenly browned.
2. Add the onions, peppers, garlic, ginger, cinnamon and 6 lemon slices. Cover and cook over low heat for 10 minutes.
3. Add 2½ cups water, cover and simmer until the chicken is nearly tender – about 15 minutes.

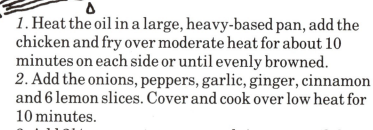

4. Add the potatoes, almonds and olives, cover and simmer for another 15 minutes.

CONQUEROR'S GAME BIRD

We invented this to celebrate the 900th anniversary of England's *Domesday Book*, commissioned by William the Conqueror. We have used ingredients which William's cooks would have had to hand.

3-3½ lb broiler-fryer
2 carrots, chopped
1 onion, chopped
2 cloves of garlic, chopped
3 bay leaves
sprigs of fresh thyme, marjoram and basil
6 peppercorns, crushed
6 juniper berries, crushed

2 teaspoons salt
2 tablespoons vinegar
2½ cups red wine
4 tablespoons butter
2 tablespoons flour

Marinating 4 days
Preparation 10 minutes
Cooking 2 hours 35 minutes
Temperature 275°F

MENU PLANNING: Serve with wild rice and a mixed green salad.
Drink a good claret, or Cabernet from California.

1. Put the chicken into a bowl that it just fits, pack the vegetables, herbs and spices around, sprinkle on the salt and vinegar and pour over enough wine to more than half cover it.
2. Keep in the refrigerator and turn daily for 4 days.
3. Remove the chicken and pat it dry. Strain the marinade and discard solids.
4. Melt the butter in a large skillet, add the chicken and cook over moderate heat for 15-20 minutes or until evenly brown all over. Remove the chicken.
5. Stir the flour into the skillet, then gradually stir in 2½ cups of the strained marinade and heat until it thickens to a thin sauce.
6. Put the chicken in an ovenproof casserole, pour the sauce over, cover and bake for 2 hours at 275°F, or at the lowest temperature at which your oven functions efficiently.
7. Remove the chicken and keep warm on a serving dish.
8. Boil the liquid for 10-15 minutes or until reduced to a thickish sauce. Pour half over the chicken and serve the rest separately.

CHICKEN WITH 40 BAY LEAVES

A dish for anyone with a flourishing bay tree who can never think of enough uses for the leaves. If you don't have a bay tree, dried bay leaves will also give good results.

2 tablespoons olive oil
4 tablespoons butter
40 bay leaves
5 cloves of garlic, crushed
½ cup flour
salt and black pepper
3-3½ lb broiler-fryer, cut up (see page 13)
⅔ cup heavy cream
juice of 1 lemon
2 tablespoons brandy or grappa

Preparation 10 minutes
Cooking 1 hour 45 minutes
Temperature 300°F

MENU PLANNING: Serve with mashed potatoes and baked onions.
Drink a dry red wine, say Chianti.

1. Heat the oil and butter in a large skillet, then add the bay leaves and garlic and fry over moderate heat for about 5 minutes or until crisp.
2. Season the flour with salt and pepper and use to coat the chicken parts.
3. Push the bay leaves and garlic to one side and fry the chicken in the same pan over moderate heat for about 10 minutes each side or until evenly browned.
4. Transfer the chicken, bay leaves and juices to an ovenproof casserole, cover and bake for 1¼ hours at 300°F.*
5. Remove the chicken and keep warm.
6. Stir the cream and lemon juice into the casserole and reheat over low heat. Do not boil or remove the bay leaves.
7. Pour over the chicken.
8. Heat the brandy or grappa in a ladle or tablespoon over a naked flame until it ignites and pour over the chicken before serving.

ARGENTINA

This Argentinian recipe, which includes the liver and heart of the chicken, depends for its characteristic flavor on cumin and cinnamon.

3-3½ lb broiler-fryer
1 tablespoon vinegar
1 tablespoon lemon juice
1 clove of garlic, crushed
4 tablespoons butter
2 cups chopped green peppers
2 cups chopped onions
1 teaspoon ground cumin
1 teaspoon ground cinnamon
3-4 teaspoons chopped fresh herbs – sage, thyme, marjoram and chives

salt and black pepper
1 cup chopped ham
chicken's liver and heart, chopped
4 eggs, beaten
¼ cup fresh white breadcrumbs

Marinating 3 hours
Preparation 25 minutes
Cooking 1 hour 30 minutes
Temperature 375°F

MENU PLANNING: Serve with potatoes Anna and lima beans or zucchini.
Drink a South American red wine.

1. Marinate the chicken for 3 hours in 1 quart water, the vinegar, lemon juice and garlic.
2. Transfer the chicken to a large saucepan, almost cover with the marinade, bring to the boil, cover, turn down the heat and simmer gently for 45 minutes.
3. Remove the chicken, allow it to cool slightly, then remove the skin and take the flesh from the bones.
4. Melt 1 tablespoon butter in a skillet, add the peppers and onions and fry over moderate heat for about 5 minutes or until soft.
5. Stir in the cumin, cinnamon, herbs, salt, pepper, ham and the chicken's liver and heart.
6. Stir in the eggs and heat for 2-3 minutes or until they start to set.
7. Put a layer of this mixture in an ovenproof casserole, then add a layer of chicken meat, and continue to alternate the layers until both are used up, ending with the egg mixture.
8. Top with the breadcrumbs and small pieces of the remaining butter.
9. Bake for 20 minutes at 375°F.

LE VRAI COQ AU VIN*

Undistinguished attempts at Coq au vin must outnumber all other culinary disappointments. This magnificent and apparently simple dish is hard to cook well. The main problem is a sauce that is too thin. The solution is *not* to use less wine, *nor* to thicken it with more flour, but to reduce the wine by boiling before you start. This is more important than using a fine wine. Any ordinary red wine will do.

1 bottle red wine
4 bay leaves
2 sprigs of fresh thyme or 1 teaspoon of dried thyme
2 cloves of garlic, crushed
1 carrot, chopped
8 slices of bacon, diced
12-16 small onions
3-3½ lb broiler-fryer, cut up (see page 13)
2 tablespoons butter
2 tablespoons brandy
4 ounces fresh mushroom caps
½ tablespoon flour
salt and pepper
For serving
4 small slices of fried bread

Preparation 10 minutes
Cooking 1 hour 30 minutes

MENU PLANNING: Serve with plain boiled potatoes and green beans.
Drink the same kind of wine that has been used in the recipe.

1. Boil the wine in an uncovered saucepan with 2 bay leaves, 1 sprig of thyme, 1 clove of garlic and the carrot for 15-20 minutes or until reduced by half. Strain and discard the solids.
2. Cook the bacon and the onions in a large, heavy saucepan over moderate heat, stirring occasionally, until the onions start to color.
3. Remove the onions and bacon with a slotted spoon, add the chicken parts and fry over moderate heat for about 10 minutes on each side or until evenly browned, adding a little butter if necessary to prevent sticking.
4. Heat the brandy, a tablespoon at a time, over a naked flame until it ignites, then pour over the chicken.
5. Return the onions and bacon to the pan. Pour in the reduced wine, add a sprig of thyme, the remaining garlic and bay leaves, and simmer, covered, for 20 minutes.

6. Turn the chicken parts and cook for 15 minutes.
7. Add the mushrooms and cook for 5 minutes.
8. Transfer the chicken, mushrooms, onions and bacon to a warmed serving dish and keep warm.
9. Blend 1 tablespoon butter with the flour. Stir in a little sauce, then pour back into the saucepan and bring to the boil, stirring. Turn down the heat and simmer for 2 minutes.
10. Taste for seasoning, pour over the chicken and serve with small slices of fried bread.

AVOCADO RAGOÛT

A rich and spicy French method of combining chicken with avocado.

3-3½ lb broiler-fryer, cut up (see page 13)
salt and black pepper
4 tablespoons butter
1 cup chopped onions
½ teaspoon curry powder

1¼ cups chicken stock (see page 22)
2 ripe avocados
pinch of cayenne
2 tablespoons heavy cream

Preparation 15 minutes
Cooking 1 hour

MENU PLANNING: Serve with fried potatoes and a lettuce and chicory salad. Drink a dry white wine.

1. Season the chicken parts with salt and pepper.
2. Heat 2 tablespoons butter in a large skillet and fry the onions over a moderate heat for about 10 minutes on each side or until lightly colored. Add the chicken parts and cook for about 10 minutes on each side or until evenly browned – stir occasionally to prevent the onions burning.
3. Sprinkle the curry powder into the pan, add the stock, cover, turn the heat to low and simmer for 30 minutes. Remove the chicken and keep warm. Reserve the juices.
4. Meanwhile, cut the firmer parts of the avocados into ½ inch cubes. Reserve the rest.
5. Melt the remaining butter in a small saucepan, add the avocado cubes and season with salt, pepper and a pinch of cayenne. Stir gently, cover and cook over a low heat for 5 minutes, shaking the pan occasionally to prevent the avocado sticking.
6. Blend the remaining avocado flesh with the cream, then stir in the chicken juices and beat for 2-3 minutes. Pour over the avocado cubes and cook over low heat for 2-3 minutes. Do not boil.
7. Place the chicken on a serving dish and pour the avocado mixture over.

COLD CHICKEN PIE

This pie is good hot but even better cold when the sauce has jellied.

2½-3 lb broiler, cut up (see page 13)
4-5 stalks of celery, chopped
2 onions, chopped
12 black peppercorns
3 or 4 sprigs of fresh thyme or 1 teaspoon dried thyme
½ teaspoon grated nutmeg
salt
For the pie crust
1 cup all-purpose flour
salt
½ cup butter or margarine

2 cups fresh chopped mushrooms
1½ tablespoons butter
1 lb bacon slices
4 or 5 sprigs fresh parsley, chopped

Preparation 30 minutes
Stock 45 minutes
Cooling stock 1 hour
Cooking 1 hour
Cooling pie 3 hours
Temperature 350°F

MENU PLANNING: Serve with coleslaw. Drink beer.

1. Put the chicken parts, celery, onions, peppercorns, thyme, nutmeg and salt into a saucepan, cover with cold water, cover the pan and bring to the boil, then turn down the heat and simmer until tender – about 45 minutes.
2. For the pie crust, sift the flour and salt into a bowl, add the butter or margarine and rub into the flour until the mixture resembles breadcrumbs. Sprinkle over approximately 2 tablespoons water and mix to form a dough. Cover and chill for 30 minutes.
3. Remove the chicken from the pan and allow to cool slightly before removing the skin and taking the meat off the bones.
4. Strain the stock and leave until cold, then remove all the fat from the surface.
5. Meanwhile, melt the butter in a skillet and cook the mushrooms over a moderate heat for about 10 minutes to extract their juices. Drain them thoroughly.
6. Layer the chicken, bacon and mushrooms in a 9-inch pie plate, sprinkling parsley and salt and pepper between the layers. Pour in enough stock to just cover.

7. Roll out the pie crust on a lightly floured surface to the same shape as the pie plate, but slightly larger. Cut a strip from around the edge of the dough, place it on the rim of the plate and dampen it. Place the remaining dough on the plate and press the edges lightly onto the lining strip. Make a small slit in the center with the point of a sharp knife. Bake for 35 minutes at 350°F.
8. Cool for 3 hours.

TUNISIAN SALAD

A simple salad for which you can use leftover rice, but it is more interesting if you prepare the special flavored rice that we describe.

1 tablespoon oil
1½ cups long-grain rice
½ cup finely chopped onion
¼ cup golden raisins
¼ cup sliced almonds
¼ teaspoon ground cinnamon
3 ripe tomatoes each cut into 8 pieces

3 cups chopped cold cooked chicken
2-3 tablespoons Italian salad dressing
1 lettuce

Preparation 15 minutes
Cooking 20 minutes
Cooling 2 hours

MENU PLANNING: Serve with cheese, relishes and pickles.
Drink Vinho Verde.

1. Heat the oil in a heavy-based saucepan, add the rice and onion and cook over moderate heat for about 5 minutes or until the rice is translucent.
2. Stir in the golden raisins, almonds, cinnamon and 3 cups water. Bring to the boil, cover, turn down the heat and simmer until the water is absorbed – 12-14 minutes.
3. Leave until cold, uncovered.
4. Mix the tomatoes, chicken and salad dressing into the cold rice.
5. Serve surrounded by lettuce leaves.

MIRACLE CHICKEN

The important points to watch in this very simple way of cooking chicken are that you have a pan that will hold the chicken plus its skewers (these conduct the heat), that the water covers the chicken and that the lid is not lifted until the chicken is cold. If using a frozen bird make sure it is thoroughly, and freshly, thawed. Always check that the meat is cooked. The juices must be clear when the flesh is pierced with a skewer. You can serve the chicken simply with a sprinkling of soy sauce or with the Provençal sauce given below.

3-3½ lb broiler-fryer
4 tablespoons wine vinegar
4 slices of ginger root
1 cup chopped scallions
salt
For the sauce
½ cup finely chopped onion
½ teaspoon chopped fresh parsley or a small pinch of dried parsley
2 anchovies, finely chopped

1½ tablespoons capers, finely chopped
2 hard-cooked egg yolks, chopped
1 egg yolk
1 cup olive oil
juice of 1 lemon

Preparation 10 minutes
Cooking 10 minutes
Cooling 4 hours
Sauce 20 minutes

MENU PLANNING: Serve with a potato salad. Drink a dry white wine.

1. Push 4 metal skewers through the chicken from side to side.
2. Rub some of the vinegar over the chicken and pour the rest into a large pan with the ginger, scallions, a little salt and enough water to cover the chicken.
3. Bring to the boil, add the chicken, bring back to the boil, turn down the heat and simmer for only 30 seconds.
4. Turn off the heat and leave until completely cold, about 4 hours. The chicken will then be cooked.
5. For the sauce, mix together the onion, parsley, anchovies and capers with the hard-cooked egg yolks, then stir in the raw egg yolk.

6. Stir in the olive oil and lemon juice a few drops at a time.
7. Remove the cold chicken from the pan and carve it into slices. Serve accompanied by the sauce.

COUNTRY SALAD

This simple but excellent salad depends on fresh crisp lettuce and homemade mayonnaise.

For the mayonnaise
2 small egg yolks
½ teaspoon dry mustard powder
salt
pinch of cayenne
⅓ cup olive oil
1 tablespoon white wine vinegar
For the salad
3 cups diced cooked chicken
1 lb can bean sprouts
2 stalks of celery, diced
1 tablespoon French salad dressing
1 teaspoon soy sauce
For serving
1 large crisp lettuce
1 cup pitted green olives

Preparation 20-25 minutes
Cooking none

MENU PLANNING: Serve with rye bread and scallions. Drink white wine.

1. For the mayonnaise, beat together the egg yolks, mustard, salt and cayenne, then very slowly beat in the oil to make a thick sauce. Beat in the vinegar.
2. Mix the chicken, bean sprouts and celery together, then toss in the French dressing and sprinkle on the soy sauce.
3. Mix the chicken mixture with the mayonnaise and serve on a bed of lettuce and top with green olives.

HOENDER PASTEI

All too often a chicken pie contains a thin and uninteresting sauce. In this excellent and unusual recipe from South Africa the chicken is cooked separately so the juices can be reduced and added at the last minute.

3-3½ lb broiler-fryer, skinned and cut up (see page 13)
chicken's skin
½ teaspoon mace
1 teaspoon ground allspice
salt and black pepper
2½ cups chicken stock (see page 22)
For the pie crust
1½ cups self-rising flour
salt
5 tablespoons lard or butter, diced

2 hard-boiled eggs, sliced
2-4 ounces ham, sliced
2-4 ounces fresh mushrooms, sliced if necessary
1 tablespoon flour

Preparation 45 minutes
Cooking 1 hour 30 minutes
Temperature 425°F
Cooling 3 hours

> MENU PLANNING: Serve with a mixed salad. Drink a dry white wine.

1. Simmer the chicken and skin with the mace, allspice, salt and pepper in the stock in a covered saucepan over moderate heat until tender – about 30 minutes.
2. For the pie crust, sift the flour and salt into a bowl and cut in the lard or butter. Mix to a dough with about 2 tablespoons cold water. Knead lightly, then cover and leave in the refrigerator for 30 minutes.
3. Remove the chicken from the stock, allow to cool a little, then remove the flesh from the bones.
4. Arrange alternate layers of chicken, egg, ham and mushrooms in a 9-inch pie plate. The plate should be well filled to support the crust.
5. Roll out the dough on a lightly floured surface to the same shape as the pie plate, but slightly larger. Cut a strip from around the edge of the dough, place on the rim of the pie dish and dampen it. Place the remaining dough over the pie plate. Lightly press the edge of the dough onto the lining strip. Make a small

hole in the center of the pie crust with the point of a sharp knife.

6. Bake for about 20 minutes at 425°F until the pastry is a light golden brown.

7. Meanwhile, blend the tablespoon of flour with a little of the stock and boil the rest of the stock for about 15 minutes or until reduced to 1¼ cups.

8. Gradually stir some of the hot stock into the blended flour, then pour it back into the pan and boil, stirring constantly, for 5-10 minutes or until thickened.

9. Pour the thickened stock into the hole in the pie crust and leave until cold, about 3 hours.

NUTTY CHEF'S SALAD

A rich salad with an interesting combination of tastes. An excellent way of using leftover chicken.

2-3 cups cooked chicken
1 cup chopped ham
1 cup chopped Gruyère or Emmental cheese
1 cup cashew nuts

For the mayonnaise
½ teaspoon dry mustard
salt and pepper
1 egg yolk, beaten
⅔ cup olive oil
2 teaspoons wine vinegar
a few drops Worcestershire sauce

Preparation 15-20 minutes
Cooking none

MENU PLANNING: Serve with a green salad and wholewheat bread. Drink a dry fruity white wine.

1. Mix the chicken, ham, cheese and nuts together.
2. For the mayonnaise, blend the mustard, salt and pepper into the egg yolk, then add the oil, a few drops at a time, beating continuously.
3. When all the oil has been added and the mayonnaise is stiff and shiny, mix in the vinegar and a few drops of Worcestershire sauce.
4. Stir the mayonnaise into the chicken mixture.

CURRIED CREAMED CHICKEN

This is mainly a way of using leftover cooked chicken, but it is so good that it is worth cooking a chicken especially for the purpose.

1¼ cups heavy cream
¼ cup light cream
2-4 teaspoons curry powder, to taste
salt and black pepper
4 cooked chicken parts or a cooked 3-3½ lb broiler-fryer, quartered

Preparation 15 minutes
Cooking none

> MENU PLANNING: Serve with cold potatoes and green beans in a vinaigrette. Drink beer.

1. Mix together the creams, curry powder and salt and pepper.
2. Dip the chicken parts into the cream mixture and place on a serving dish. Pour over any of the cream that is left.

POLLO IN SALSA TONNATA

This classic Italian dish is equally good when made with leftover cooked chicken or turkey.

2½-3 lb broiler or about 4 cups chopped cooked chicken or turkey
6 black peppercorns
salt and black pepper
1 tablespoon olive oil
For the tuna fish mayonnaise
3½ ounce can tuna fish in oil
4 anchovies
⅔ cup olive oil
1 tablespoon lemon juice or white wine vinegar
2 egg yolks
black pepper
1 tablespoon capers

Preparation 20 minutes
Cooking 45 minutes
Cooling 4 hours

> MENU PLANNING: Serve with hot or cold lima beans and sautéed potatoes. Drink a dry white wine, Italian if available.

1. Poach the chicken, if using, with the peppercorns in salted water in a large covered saucepan until tender – 30-45 minutes.
2. Remove the chicken and allow to cool slightly before taking off the skin and removing the meat from the bones.
3. Put the chicken meat on a plate, sprinkle with a little salt and black pepper and pour the olive oil over. Leave until cold.
4. For the tuna fish mayonnaise, mash the tuna fish and anchovies with a little olive oil or mix in a blender or food processor. Mix in the lemon juice or vinegar, egg yolks and a little pepper.
5. Gradually add the rest of the oil a drop at a time, beating after each addition.
6. Stir in the capers and pour the mayonnaise over the chicken.

CHICKEN IN ASPIC

This simple and reliable recipe makes an excellent picnic or party dish. But be careful. It is rich and you can easily eat too much.

3-3½ lb broiler-fryer
salt
10 black peppercorns
sherry or brandy, to taste (optional)
1 tablespoon gelatin dissolved in 3 tablespoons cold water

1 egg yolk, lightly beaten
⅔ cup heavy cream
cayenne, to taste

Preparation none
Cooking 2 hours
Cooling 4 hours

> MENU PLANNING: Serve with fresh raw vegetables — grated carrot, celery stalks, lettuce, cucumber or tomatoes.

1. Put the chicken, salt and peppercorns into a large saucepan and cover with cold water. Bring to the boil, turn down the heat, cover, and simmer until tender — about 35-45 minutes.

2. Remove the chicken from the water and leave to cool slightly, then discard the skin, take the meat from the bones and grind in a meat grinder or food processor.

3. To make the aspic, add 2½ cups boiling water (and a little sherry or brandy if you like) to the dissolved gelatin, then leave in a 1½ quart bowl to cool.

4. In another bowl mix the ground chicken with the egg yolk and 3 teaspoons of the warm aspic. Leave until cold.

5. Fold the cream into the chicken mixture, and add salt and cayenne to taste.

6. When the aspic in the bowl has formed into jelly about 1 inch thick around the sides, ladle out the liquid center, put in the chicken mixture, then pour the liquid over the top.

7. Leave in the refrigerator to set.

8. Turn out by dipping the bowl in hot water for a few seconds, then inverting it onto a plate.

CRÊPES TERESA

An excellent dish to make from a small amount of cooked chicken. Any kind of cheese can be used, but a hard, strong cheese like Parmesan is best. This recipe serves 6.

For the cheese sauce
4 tablespoons butter
¼ cup flour
3 cups milk
⅓ cup grated cheese
black pepper
For the filling
2 cups finely ground cooked chicken
1½ cups cooked spinach
⅓ cup grated cheese
salt
For the crêpes
1 cup all-purpose flour
salt
1 egg, beaten
1¼ cups milk
approximately 2 tablespoons oil

Preparation 10 minutes
Cooking 30 minutes

MENU PLANNING: Serve with baked onions. Drink a fruity red wine, say Beaujolais.

1. For the cheese sauce, melt the butter in a small saucepan, then stir in the flour and cook for 1 minute. Gradually stir in the milk, then bring to the boil, stirring. Lower the heat and simmer for 2 minutes, then remove from the heat and stir in the cheese and pepper.
2. For the filling, mix all the ingredients together with 1¼ cups of the sauce to make a stiff paste.
3. For the crêpes, sift the flour and salt into a bowl and make a well in the center. Drop the egg into the well, then gradually pour in the milk, stirring constantly to draw the flour into the liquid.
4. Heat a little oil in a non-stick skillet over moderate heat, add 1-2 tablespoons of the batter, tilt the pan so the batter covers the surface and cook for about 3 minutes until golden and set on the underside. Turn the crêpe over and cook the other side until browned. Remove and fill with the chicken mixture. Roll the crêpe up and place in a shallow ovenproof dish. Make 5 more crêpe rolls in the same way, adding more oil to the skillet as it is needed.
5. Cover the crêpe rolls with the remaining sauce and place under the broiler to brown.

RISOTTO ALLA MILANESE

Use either cooked chicken or cooked chicken livers for this dish. Cooked peas are a nice addition. Beef marrow is not easy to buy and you will probably have to extract some from beef bones or substitute a beef bouillon cube.

4 tablespoons butter
1 small onion, finely chopped
2 tablespoons beef marrow or 1 beef bouillon cube, crumbled
1½ cups short-grain rice
⅓ cup dry white wine
2½ cups chicken stock (see page 22)
6-8 saffron strands, crushed and steeped in a little hot stock for 5 minutes

2 tablespoons grated Parmesan cheese
2 cups chopped cooked chicken or chicken livers
salt and black pepper

Preparation 10 minutes
Cooking 40 minutes

MENU PLANNING: No vegetables needed. Drink a red or white Italian wine.

1. Melt 1 tablespoon butter in a large skillet, add the onion and cook over low heat for about 5 minutes or until softened.
2. Stir in the marrow or bouillon cube and the rice and cook, stirring, until the grains become translucent.
3. Stir in the wine and increase the heat. Boil for 5-7 minutes or until nearly all the liquid has evaporated.
4. Stir in the stock, stir once, cover and simmer for 15 minutes or until the liquid has been absorbed and the rice is tender.
5. Stir in the saffron and soaking liquid, cheese and remaining butter, then place the chicken or chicken livers on top for about 5 minutes to heat through.
6. Stir all the ingredients together and taste for seasoning.

SWEET AND SOUR CHICKEN

The sweet and sour sauce can be prepared ahead; the final stages of the recipe take about five minutes.

For the sauce
1 tablespoon oil
2 tablespoons wine vinegar
2-3 teaspoons sugar
salt
1 lb can crushed pineapple, drained
2 tablespoons cornstarch

For the chicken
2-3 cups chopped cooked chicken
1 egg, beaten
2 tablespoons cornstarch
2 tablespoons oil

Preparation 5 minutes
Cooking 25 minutes

> MENU PLANNING: Serve with boiled rice and broccoli or cauliflower. Drink Chinese tea.

1. For the sauce, bring the oil, vinegar, sugar, salt and 2 tablespoons water boiling point in a saucepan.
2. Add the pineapple.
3. Blend the cornstarch with 2 tablespoons water, stir into the pineapple mixture and cook over low heat for 5-10 minutes, stirring, until it thickens.
4. Mix together the chicken and egg.
5. Sprinkle on the cornstarch and stir together.
6. Heat the oil in a skillet, add the chicken and fry over high heat for 2-3 minutes, until it begins to become crisp.
7. Drain the chicken on paper towels, then stir into the sauce and cook over low heat for 2 minutes. If the sauce seems too thick, add some pineapple juice.

BREADED CHICKEN PATTIES

This economical dish uses leftover cooked rice as well as cooked chicken.

2 tablespoons butter
2 tablespoons flour
2/3 cup chicken stock (see page 22)
2 cups finely chopped cooked chicken
1/2 cup boiled long-grain rice

2 heaping teaspoons capers
salt and black pepper
1/2 cup dry breadcrumbs
4 tablespoons oil

Preparation 5 minutes
Chilling 1 hour
Cooking 25 minutes

> MENU PLANNING: Serve with mashed potatoes and peas.
> Drink beer.

1. Melt the butter in a heavy-based saucepan, stir in the flour, then gradually stir in the stock and bring to the boil, stirring. Turn down the heat and simmer for 2 minutes.
2. Stir the chicken, rice, capers, salt and pepper into the sauce. Leave to cool for about 30 minutes.
3. Spoon large tablespoonfuls, one at a time, onto the breadcrumbs and turn them until evenly coated. Shape into patties and refrigerate for about 30 minutes or until firm.
4. Heat the oil in a skillet, add the patties and fry over moderate heat for about 7-8 minutes on each side.
5. Drain on paper towels.

CHICKEN IN BAKED APPLES

This Arabian dish is too exotic for some friends who claim not to know whether they are eating a main course or a dessert, but we find it delicious. It is important to hollow out the apples as we describe.

4 large cooking apples, cored
6 tablespoons butter
¼ cup cooked rice
1 cup diced cooked chicken
¼ cup golden raisins
½ teaspoon ground cinnamon

1 hard-cooked egg, diced
2 teaspoons honey

Preparation 25 minutes
Cooking 30 minutes
Temperature 350°F

> MENU PLANNING: Serve with boiled rice and baked tomatoes.
> Drink beer.

1. Using an apple corer or a small, sharp knife, enlarge the hollows in the apples to at least the size of a golf ball.
2. Melt 4 tablespoons butter in a flameproof baking pan and add the apples.
3. Melt the remaining butter.
4. Divide the rice, then the melted butter among the hollows in the apples.
5. Mix the chicken, golden raisins, cinnamon and hard-cooked egg together and spoon the mixture into the apples.
6. Top each apple with ½ teaspoon honey.
7. Bake for 30 minutes at 350°F, basting with the melted butter every 10 minutes.

CHICKEN HASH

The secrets of this delicious farmhouse recipe are to add enough stock and to use plenty of oil for frying. If, nevertheless, the "cake" breaks apart, just stir all the ingredients together and serve. It will still taste good.

3 cups finely diced cooked chicken
3 cups finely diced boiled potatoes
6-8 tablespoons chicken stock (see page 22)

salt and black pepper
4 tablespoons oil
3 onions, sliced

Preparation 10 minutes
Cooking 25 minutes

> MENU PLANNING: Serve with corn and a green salad. Drink beer.

1. Mix together the chicken, potatoes, stock, salt and pepper to form a thick, creamy mixture.
2. Heat the oil in a large skillet, add the onions and fry over moderate heat for about 7 minutes or until they begin to color.
3. Add the chicken mixture, pat it down flat and fry over moderate heat for about 15 minutes or until the bottom is crisp.
4. Fold the "cake" over like an omelet and serve.

CHICKEN RICE CASSEROLE

This modestly titled recipe makes a similar but more economical dish than the risotto on page 117.

½ cup chopped onion
1½ cups rice
2½ cups chicken stock (see page 22)
¼ cup grated cheese
¼ cup golden raisins, optional

salt and black pepper
2 cups chopped cooked chicken
2 tablespoons butter

Preparation 5 minutes
Cooking 45 minutes
Temperature 350°F

> MENU PLANNING: No vegetables needed. Drink an ordinary red or white wine.

1. Stir all the ingredients together in an ovenproof casserole.
2. Cover and bake for 45 minutes at 350°F.

JUTLAND BLUE

Our cousin, Sebastian, who is one-quarter Danish, brought back this delicious method of using cooked chicken. In Jutland they, of course, use the local cheese, but any Danish blue cheese can be substituted.

1 tablespoon butter
1 cup fresh chopped mushrooms
2 cloves of garlic, crushed
2½ cups finely chopped cooked chicken
1 egg
1 teaspoon caraway seeds
salt and black pepper
6 large thin slices of boiled ham

For the sauce
3 tablespoons butter
½ cup flour
2½ cups milk
1½ cups grated or finely crumbled Jutland or other Danish blue cheese
black pepper

Preparation 10 minutes
Cooking 40 minutes
Temperature 350°F

MENU PLANNING: Begin with Danish herrings and straight aquavit. Drink beer.

1. Melt the butter in a skillet, add the mushrooms and garlic and fry over moderate heat for about 5 minutes or until just soft, stirring occasionally.
2. Stir in the chicken, egg, caraway seeds, salt and pepper.
3. Divide the chicken among the slices of ham. Roll the slices up and place side by side in a flat, shallow baking dish.
4. For the sauce, melt the butter in a saucepan, stir in the flour and cook, stirring, for 1 minute, then gradually stir in the milk. Bring to the boil, still stirring, then turn down the heat and simmer for 2 minutes. Remove from the heat and stir in 1 cup of the cheese and the pepper.
5. Pour the sauce over the ham rolls and top with the remaining cheese.
6. Bake for 20 minutes at 350°F, then brown under the broiler.

STUFFED EGGPLANTS

We describe the basic method, and give a mixture of ingredients which make a good filling, but these can be almost infinitely varied.

2 eggplants, each about ½-¾ lb
4 tablespoons butter
½ cup chopped onion
½ cup fresh chopped mushrooms
2 tomatoes, peeled and chopped
1 clove of garlic, crushed
2 cups finely ground cooked chicken
½ cup cooked rice
1 tablespoon tomato paste

½ cup grated cheese
salt and black pepper
½ cup fresh breadcrumbs

Preparation 10 minutes
Cooking 1 hour
Temperature 350°F

MENU PLANNING: Serve with fried potatoes and sautéed red peppers. Drink a red Greek wine.

1. Cut the eggplants in half lengthwise and simmer, cut-side down, in a little water in a large covered pan for about 20 minutes.
2. Meanwhile, melt 2 tablespoons butter in a saucepan, add the onion, mushrooms and tomatoes and cook over low heat for about 10 minutes or until soft, stirring occasionally.
3. Remove the eggplants from the water, and allow them to drain well. Place the eggplants cut-side up in a baking dish and scoop out the flesh with a teaspoon, but using a knife to cut through the fibers at the stalk end. Take care not to break the skin.
4. Chop the eggplant and mix it with the onion, mushrooms and tomatoes, then stir in the garlic, chicken, rice, tomato paste, grated cheese, salt and pepper. If the mixture seems dry, moisten it with a little stock or water.
5. Spoon the filling into the eggplant shells, then dot with the remaining butter and sprinkle the breadcrumbs evenly over the tops.
6. Bake for 20 minutes at 350°F, then place under the broiler for a few minutes to brown.

CHICKEN NEWBURG

This is similar to the better-known Lobster Newburg. It should be made with chicken that has been cooked by a simple method, or the delicate flavor of the Newburg will be spoiled.

6 tablespoons rendered chicken fat or butter
1 cup fresh sliced mushrooms
5 cups chopped cooked chicken
½ cup dry sherry
⅓ cup light cream

3 egg yolks, beaten
salt and black pepper
For serving
6 slices of toast
paprika

Preparation 10 minutes
Cooking 30 minutes

MENU PLANNING: Drink a light white wine.

1. Melt the chicken fat or butter in a skillet, add the mushrooms and cook over low heat for about 5 minutes or until just softened.
2. Add the chicken and half the sherry and cook for 2-3 minutes.
3. Transfer the mixture to a double boiler or to a bowl over a saucepan of simmering water, stir in the cream and heat, stirring occasionally, for 2-3 minutes.
4. Blend the egg yolks with a little of the warm cooking juices, then stir them into the chicken mixture with the remaining sherry.
5. Continue to cook over low heat, stirring, for 5-10 minutes or until the sauce thickens.
6. Add salt and pepper to taste. Serve on hot toast sprinkled with paprika.

CANNELLONI

Although we don't pretend that our chicken cannelloni is the genuine thing it is nevertheless extremely good, and a convenient way of using up a small quantity of cold chicken. This dish will serve 6.

2 tablespoons butter
½ cup finely chopped onion
3 ounces chicken livers
1½ cups finely chopped cooked chicken
1 egg
½ cup grated Parmesan cheese
salt and black pepper

12 squares fresh pasta or 12 cannelloni tubes, boiled and drained
⅔ cup chicken stock (see page 22)

Preparation 15 minutes
Cooking 35 minutes
Temperature 350°F

MENU PLANNING: Serve with a tossed salad. Drink Chianti.

1. Melt half the butter in a skillet, add the onion and fry over moderate heat for about 5 minutes or until softened.
2. Add the chicken livers and fry for 2 minutes.
3. Mash the onions and liver together, then mix with the chicken, egg, half the cheese, salt and pepper.
4. Wrap this mixture in the pasta squares, or fill the tubes. Do not pack them too tightly or they will be heavy.
5. With the remaining butter grease an ovenproof dish that the cannelloni will almost fill. Lay the stuffed cannelloni side by side in the dish.
6. Bring the stock almost to boiling point and pour over the cannelloni.
7. Sprinkle with the remaining cheese.
8. Cover and bake for 15 minutes at 350°F.
9. Uncover and brown lightly under the broiler.

GALANTINE PARFAIT

Not only does this taste extremely good but it looks magnificent when served and carved. Practice first before serving it at a dinner party as it may take you well over half an hour to bone the bird and your initial attempt may not look as good as you would like it to. It is also delicious cold.

3-3½ lb broiler-fryer, boned (see page 14, Method A)
For the stuffing
8 ounces chicken livers, roughly chopped
1 cup fresh roughly chopped mushrooms
¾ cup heavy cream
1 cup fresh white breadcrumbs
1 heaping tablespoon chopped fresh parsley or 1½ tablespoons dried parsley
3 teaspoons fresh thyme or 1½ teaspoons dried thyme
1 teaspoon lemon juice
1 clove of garlic, crushed
salt and black pepper
6 tablespoons butter, melted
1 egg, beaten

Preparation 1 hour 30 minutes
Cooking 1 hour 30 minutes
Temperature 375°F

> MENU PLANNING: Serve with spinach salad in Italian dressing.
> Drink a light red wine.

1. For the stuffing, mix the chicken livers, mushrooms, cream, breadcrumbs, herbs, lemon juice, garlic, salt and pepper with the melted butter.
2. Bind together with the beaten egg.
3. First put a little stuffing into the wings and legs, then spread the remainder over the central cavity, being careful to distribute it evenly.
4. Fold the loose skin over the openings and tie the legs and wings into place, re-forming the shape of the unboned bird.
5. Place the chicken in a casserole or small roasting pan that will hold it in shape.
6. Roast for 1 hour 20 minutes at 375°F.
7. Leave the chicken in the casserole or pan for 10 minutes before transferring to a warmed carving dish. Cut in thick slices to serve.

INDEX

almond: chicken in almond sauce, 70
  gallina en pepitoria, 62
  Moroccan chicken, 98
  Persian pilaf, 66-7
anchovy: pollo in salsa tonnata, 113
  sauté aux olives, 94
apple: chicken in baked apples, 119
  Normandy chicken, 53
apricots: chicken Marengo, 50
Argentina, 101
aspic, chicken in, 114
avocado ragoût, 104

bacon: cold chicken pie, 106-7
  pollo al latte, 72
  terrine maison, 36
bay, chicken with 40 bay leaves, 100
bean sprouts: Cantonese chicken, 46
  country salad, 109
  crisp and smooth, 46
Béarnais, chicken, 97
blanquette de poule, 68
boiling fowl, 10
boiling, 16
boning chickens, 14-15
breast cutlets, 15
brine, salting in, 19-20
broiled chicken Maintenon, 92
broiler-fryers, 9
broiling, 16-17
buying chickens, 10-11

Calvados: Normandy chicken, 53
  Vallé d'Auge, 78
cannelloni, 124
Cantonese chicken, 46
capers: breaded chicken patties, 118-19
  miracle chicken, 108-9
carving, 18
cashew nuts: nutty chef's salad, 112
  kaju murgh kari, 69
casserole, baking in, 17

chicken in almond sauce, 70
chicken Chinoise, 80
chicken fricassée, 60
chicken Marengo, 50
chicken Newburg, 123
chicken paprika, 71
chicken Provençal, 95
chicken with 40 bay leaves, 100
chopped liver, 37
cinnamon chicken, 65
Conqueror's game bird, 99
gallina en pepitoria, 62
Mexican chowder, 86
mushroom casserole, 57
Normandy chicken, 53
sauté à la paysanne, 59
sweet and spicy chicken, 55
Vallé d'Auge, 78
Le vrai coq au vin, 102-3
waterzooi, 64
West African peanut stew, 52
see also curry
celestial chicken, 73
cheese: cannelloni, 124
  chicken cheese balls, 82
  crêpes Teresa, 116
  Jutland blue, 121
  nutty chef's salad, 112
  Parmesan chicken, 48
  risotto alla Milanese, 117
  sauce, 116
  stuffed egg plants, 122
chick peas, sopa picadillo, 30
chicken bedsprings, 44
chicken cheese balls, 89
chicken hash, 120
Chinoise, chicken, 80
chowder: corn, 26
  Mexican chicken, 86
cider: chicken Chinoise, 80
  Vallé d'Auge, 78
cinnamon chicken, 65
cock-a-leekie, 24
coconut, Senegal chicken, 96
cold chicken pie, 106-7
cold dishes, 105-14
Conqueror's game bird, 99
consommé, 23
cooking methods, 16-17
coq au vin, 102-3
corn chowder, 26

country salad, 109
crab and chicken, 51
cream: chicken in aspic, 114
  chicken Newburg, 123
  chicken with 40 bay leaves, 100
  curried creamed chicken, 112-13
  gourmet Hongroise, 87
  Normandy chicken, 53
  poussin with sour cream, 58
  Vallé d'Auge, 78
cream cheese: celestial chicken, 73
  mousse, 41
creamed chicken soup, 27
crêpes Teresa, 116
crisp and smooth, 46
crostini, 39
croûtons, 30
curry: curried creamed chicken, 112-13
curried fritos, 40-1
  kaju murgh kari, 69
  Nairobi curry, 54
cutlets, 15

drawing chickens, 12
drumstick cutlets, 15

egg: piperade with chicken livers, 75
eggplant: stuffed, 122

farmhouse roast chicken, 56-7
feather fowlie, 28
food value, 9
fresh chickens, 10-11
fricassée, 60
fritos, curried, 40-1
frozen chickens, 10, 12-13, 18-19
frying, 17

galantine parfait, 125
gallina en pebre, 76-7
gallina en pepitoria, 62

126

ginger: chicken Chinoise, 80
   miracle chicken, 108-9
gourmet Hongroise, 87

ham: Argentina, 101
   Hoender pastei, 110-11
   Jutland blue, 121
   nutty chef's salad, 112
   pâté-terrine de volaille, 38-9
hearty lentil soup, 25
Hoender pastei, 110-11

Jutland blue, 121

kaju murgh kari, 69
Kiev, chicken, 93

leek: cock-a-leekie, 24
   white cloud, 84
lemon: lemon and orange chicken, 49
   Parmesan chicken, 48
   salted, for Moroccan chicken, 98
lentils, hearty soup, 25
liver, 11
   cannelloni, 124
   chicken liver pâté, 35
   chicken livers Madeira, 47
   chopped liver, 37
   crisp and smooth, 46
crostini, 39
   galantine parfait, 125
   piperade with, 75
   pollo pisto, 79
   risotto alla Milanese, 117
   simple pâté, 34
   terrine maison, 36
   terrine with pork, 42

Madeira, chicken livers Madeira, 47
mandarin velvet, 74
Marengo, chicken, 50
mayonnaise: nutty chef's salad, 112
   country salad, 109

pollo in salsa tonnata, 113
Mexican chicken, 86
microwave ovens, 17
milk, pollo al latte, 72
miracle chicken, 108-9
mizutaki, 63
Moroccan chicken, 98
mousse, cream cheese, 41
mushroom: blanquette de poule, 68
   broiled chicken Maintenon, 92
   chicken fricassée, 60
   chicken Marengo, 50
   chicken Newburg, 123
   chicken Provençal, 95
   cold chicken pie, 106-7
   galantine parfait, 125
   Hoender pastei, 110-11
   Jutland blue, 121
   mandarin velvet, 74
   mushroom casserole, 57
   stuffed eggplants, 122
   Le vrai coq au vin, 102-3
mussels, paella, 89

Nairobi curry, 54
Normandy chicken, 53
nutty chef's salad, 112

olives: country salad, 109
   Mexican chicken, 86
   Moroccan chicken, 98
   sauté aux olives, 94
onion: rijsttafel, 85
   Le vrai coq au vin, 102-3
orange and lemon chicken, 49
Oriental grilled wings, 81
oven temperatures, 8

paella, 89
paprika, chicken, 71
Parmesan chicken, 48
parsnip and chicken soup, 31
parts, chicken, 11, 13-14
pasta, chicken bedsprings, 44
pastry, 110-11
pâtés: chicken liver, 35
   chopped liver, 87

crostini, 39
pâté-terrine de volaille, 38-9
simple pâté, 34
terrine maison, 36
terrine with pork, 42
patties, chicken, 118-19
   curried fritos, 40-1
   Polish, 91
peanuts, West African stew, 52
peas, mandarin velvet, 74
peppers: Argentina, 101
   gourmet Hongroise, 87
   Moroccan chicken, 98
   piperade with chicken livers, 75
   West African peanut stew, 52
Persian pilaf, 66-7
pies: cold chicken pie, 106-7
   Hoender pastei, 110-11
pilaf, Persian, 66
pilau, Cape style, 45
pine nuts, pollo verde, 56
pineapple, sweet and sour chicken, 118
piperade with chicken livers, 75
plucking, 11-12
Polish patties, 91
pollo al latte, 72
pollo en salsa de huevos, 76
pollo in salsa tonnata, 113
pollo pisto, 79
pollo verde, 56
pork: pâté-terrine de volaille, 38-9
   terrine with, 42
potato: chicken hash, 120
   Moroccan chicken, 98
   sauté à la paysanne, 59
poule au pot Henri IV, 90
poussin, 9
   with sour cream, 58
prawns, paella, 89
   rijstafel, 85
preparation, 11-15
preserving methods, 18-20
Provençal, chicken, 95

rice: chicken patties, 118-19
   chicken rice casserole, 120
   paella, 89

Persian pilaf, 66-7
pilau, Cape style, 45
rijsttafel, 85
risotto alla Milanese, 117
stuffed eggplants, 122
Tunisian salad, 107
rijsttafel, 85
risotto, *see* rice
roaster, 10
roasting, 9, 16
rotisserie cooking, 16

saffron, paella, 89
Persian pilaf, 66-7
risotto alla Milanese, 117
salads: country salad, 109
nutty chef's salad, 112
Tunisian, 107
salting in brine, 19-20
sauté à la paysanne, 59
Senegal chicken, 96
shellfish, paella, 89
sopa picadillo, 30
soups, 21-32
soy sauce: mizutaki, 63

white cloud, 84
spinach, crêpes Teresa, 116
stewing hen, 10
stock, 22, 90
stuffing, 13
sweet and sour chicken, 118
sweet and spicy chicken, 55
sweetcorn: corn chowder, 26
Mexican chicken, 86

terrines, *see* pâtés
thawing chickens, 12-13
thigh cutlets, 15
tomato: chicken Marengo, 50
chicken Provençal, 95
Mexican chicken, 86
piperade with chicken livers, 75
stuffed eggplants, 122
tongue, broiled Maintenon, 92
trussing chickens, 13
tuna, pollo in salsa tonnata, 113
Tunisian salad, 107

Vallé d'Auge, 78
veal: gourmet Hongroise, 87
pâté-terrine de volaille, 38-9
velouté de volaille, 29
Le vrai coq au vin, 102-3

water chestnuts, chicken Chinoise, 80
watercress and chicken, 88
waterzooi, 64
West African peanut stew, 52
white cloud, 84
white Newburg, 123
wine: broiled chicken Maintenon, 92
chicken Marengo, 50
chicken Provençal, 95
Conqueror's game bird, 99
gallina en pepitoria, 62
sauté aux olives, 94
Le vrai coq au vin, 102-3

yogurt: chicken yogurt soup, 32
kaju murgh kari, 69